$$\frac{\text{hax med.}}{l + |^p}$$

THE SEEMING UNREALITY OF THE SPIRITUAL LIFE

THE MACMILLAN COMPANY
NEW YORK · BOSTON · CHICAGO
ATLANTA · SAN FRANCISCO

MACMILLAN & CO., Limited
LONDON · BOMBAY · CALCUTTA
MELBOURNE

THE MACMILLAN CO. OF CANADA, Ltd.
TORONTO

The Seeming Unreality of the Spiritual Life

THE
NATHANIEL WILLIAM TAYLOR LECTURES
FOR 1907

GIVEN BEFORE THE DIVINITY SCHOOL
OF YALE UNIVERSITY

BY

HENRY CHURCHILL KING

PRESIDENT OF OBERLIN COLLEGE

New York
THE MACMILLAN COMPANY
1908

COPYRIGHT, 1908
BY THE MACMILLAN COMPANY

Set up and electrotyped. Printed September, 1908

THE MASON-HENRY PRESS
SYRACUSE, N. Y.

PREFACE

This book aims to face, as straightforwardly as may be, the problem implied in its title. It seeks to speak directly, as frankly and simply as possible, and yet with some adequacy, to the fundamental religious need of men,—to the need of all who cherish ideals of any kind. The book has been written, just because this problem of the seeming unreality of the spiritual life was felt to be fundamental both for thought and life; and with the hope that considerations, that had meant much to the writer, in the solution of this problem, might not be without helpful suggestion for others. Its lines of thought might have been greatly extended, but the intention has been to treat the subject suggestively rather than exhaustively, and elaboration of thought is left to the reader.

A portion—and only a portion—of the material of the book has been given in different forms in lectures at the Harvard Summer School of Theology, at the Federate Summer School of Theology at Berkeley, California, and as the Taylor Lectures at Yale Divinity School. In the publication of these discussions it has seemed best, however, quite to abandon the lecture form. The nature of the subject has made necessary some recurrence of considerations brought out in previous books, but the argument, as presented, is intended to form an independent whole.

My indebtedness to others I have tried to make clear in the course of the discussion.

HENRY CHURCHILL KING.

Oberlin College, February, 1908.

CONTENTS

INTRODUCTION

PART I

THE CAUSES OF THE SEEMING UNREALITY

MISCONCEPTIONS

vii

viii   CONTENTS

FAILURE TO FULFIL CONDITIONS

PART II

THE WAY INTO REALITY

THE PRESUMPTIVE EVIDENCE

INTRODUCTION

I

THE FUNDAMENTAL NATURE OF THE INQUIRY

Our deepest need, always, for any ideal view or for any ideal life, is faith in the reality of the spiritual, faith in a God who can save us from being at constant war with ourselves. We all need a God, who can make rational and consistent our deepest longings, aspirations, and purposes; who can save us at least from counting as illusions all that in us which—ourselves being judges—is worthiest and most deserving to abide;—who can save us from "glorying in having renounced that which no one has ever any right to renounce."

In all this, religion does not stand alone; it makes common cause with every ideal interest and aim, of whatever kind. The aesthetic, the ethical, the philosophical, the scientific, the broadly rational of every sort, are equally concerned. Our problem is nowhere that narrow and mistaken one of the so-called "harmony of science and religion," but rather that more serious question—Have we any justifiable ideals? is there any standard for men and for life, except a pettily utilitarian one? When we think our life through to the bottom, when we carry our thought of the world to the farthest limit possible to our thinking, shall we then find our best self an illegitimate offspring of pride and error, standing naked and laid open unto that eye of reason which pierces all shams? or shall we find that rational judgment itself forced to own itself to be, in common with all other ideals, the child of faith in God, and of faith in a spiritual world whose reality we cannot doubt and continue to think at all? This is the central question of this little book.

A true theology must face this deepest question, must do something to answer this deepest need of men. A theology, therefore, that understands itself cannot be an isolated, esoteric interest of a few. Is it not rather the great attraction of theology that to it, as the science and philosophy of religion, are most directly committed the supreme interests of the race? Is it not even true that one cannot continue in philosophy *to the end,* without becoming a theologian? In a very real sense, thus, it is still possible to think of theology as "queen of the sciences," never because it seeks authoritatively to lord it anywhere, but queen because it is able to take account of the *entire* range of man's ideals, as no other science—and not even philosophy—has commonly felt free to do. In this sense, as the old schoolmen declared, theology *finds* what philosophy only seeks.

In other words, one must hold it to be the chief business of the theology of any given age or year or hour, to help to save men from "evasion of life's proof," to deliver them from shame of their best selves, to point out the conditions upon which the spiritual life may be made indubitably real. And the theme of this book thus seems to be thrust upon the theologian as demanding proof even of his right to be a worker in theology at all.

A self-respecting theologian, certainly, must always be profoundly and steadfastly unwilling to be considered the hired advocate of a little religious coterie, that can forget that the interests it defends are universal interests and meet universal needs. Is it not involved in the very conception of a religion, that it demands universal recognition? and is not this sense, as Lotze has called it, the one respectable root of fanaticism? How can the theologian, then, forget that he stands—not for the schoolmen nor for any shibboleths of the schools; not for the Fathers, nor for any ostracizing dogmas of the Fathers; but for all men and for their right and call to live the highest life, for room in which a man may stretch himself in the farthest ranges of his being, for air to breathe and light to rejoice in?

How can it be, then, that it should be particularly charged against theology, that it is unreal and binding, rather than real and setting prisoners free? That such theology, so-called, there has been, I reluctantly admit. But, nevertheless, theology belies itself, and denies its very reason for being, if it fails to be real and freeing—and freeing because it makes the spiritual life indubitably real. Our theme, thus, lies at the very heart of the theologian's problem, and, at the same time, at the heart of life. And the theologian may call artist and poet and moralist and philosopher and scientist, and every common seeker of truth and goodness and beauty, and all true lovers, to witness that in this, his quest, he fights their battles all, no less than his own.

"Does God love, and will ye hold that faith against the world?"

II

THE MEANING OF THE THEME

And what is meant by the reality of the spiritual life? How much, in the first place, should reality involve?

The value of religious opinions and experiences, it may be said with James, "can only be ascertained by spiritual judgments directly passed upon them, judgments based on our own immediate feeling primarily; and secondarily on what we can ascertain of their experimental relations to our moral needs and to the rest of what we hold as true. *Immediate luminousness,* in short, *philosophical reasonableness,* and *moral helpfulness* are the only available criteria." In other words, if the spiritual life is to be to us a real and recognized power, it must seem, first, an undoubted reality; second, to be knit up with our best thinking in other spheres; third, to have clear significance for life, as appeal and impulse to character, and as bringing enjoyment and enrichment into life. That is to say, the spiritual life must justify itself to our best judgment as real, rational, and vital. All three elements are intended to be included in the assertion of the reality of the spiritual life implied in the theme of this book.

In the spiritual life, as used in the title, it is intended to include the conviction of the fact of the Christian God and of our personal relation to him, with all that is most directly involved in these convictions.

In speaking, now, of the seeming unreality of the spiritual life, it is not, of course, intended to imply that a spiritual—that is, religious, theistic, and Christian—view of the world is ultimately less defensible than some other view. Quite the contrary. The ultimate ground and meaning of the world form a problem for any possible view that really aims to be all-embracing, for the solution of which it can only offer some hypothesis. It is not doubted that the Christian theistic hypothesis is least open to objection, when the matter is thought completely through.

But the intended suggestion of our theme is this: Probably, the great difficulty for most, in adopting the Christian point of view and coming into the Christian life, does not arise from doubt whether the Christian position is capable of a better final philosophical defense than any other position. Many would probably say that when it comes to measuring swords in logical defense of ultimate positions, the theistic and Christian view must be, no doubt, counted the victor. But that admission, though freely made, does not satisfy them. Whether with full consciousness or not, another and deeper difficulty for such minds lies behind the question of the possible philosophical defense of the Christian view. Granting that the theistic and Christian hypothesis is the best of all proposed, still they would say, why is it itself so hard to hold? Why is it not more clear and obvious? Why is so much difficulty felt by many in coming to the Christian view at all, or, at least, in justifying it rationally, after coming to it? Why is the fact of such a God as Christ reveals, and of our relations to him, not as indubitable, for example, as the existence of other persons and our relations to them? Why do not the facts of the spiritual world seem as real to us as the facts of the material world? In a word, why does the spiritual life seem often so unreal? Why is the conviction of it a wavering one with its constant ups and downs?

These are questions that press upon us from the start in every thorough-going discussion of the reality of a spiritual view and of a

spiritual life. They are there, before we begin
any of our arguments for the existence of God,
hindering the argument at every step; they are
there, after all our arguments are completed,
sapping the strength of the conviction the
arguments are supposed to bring. Men everywhere go more or less consciously under the
constant burden of the feeling that even this
best hypothesis has more difficulties than it
ought to have to be true; that especially such
a God as the Christian view affirms, and as the
heart everywhere cries out for, must have made
himself more unmistakably manifest, and not
have permitted faith to be so difficult a deed
in any case.

Some time ago, one of our religious papers[1]
furnished an illustration of this perennial question of the race about the hidden God.

"Two girls, as they walked home one night
from work, were engaged in earnest talk. A
stranger who stood on the sidewalk near them
saw the play of anxious feeling on their faces
as they stopped a moment beneath a street-
lamp's dim light. Suddenly one was heard to
say to the other, 'Yes, but why has no one ever
seen God?'—that was all, just a fragment-word

---

[1] *Sunday School Times*, April 5, 1902

throbbing with pain and regret, and they vanished again in the night.

"How like humanity that was! Like children, they pause now and then in the darkness of life, lift their weary faces to the pale lights glaring along the way, and, peering into baffled eyes, cry, 'Why can we not see our God?' It was Philip's old question, you remember, 'Show us the Father,' and all of us are now and then in Philip's class, for it is large."

The incident is a single modern echo of the ancient plaint of Job: "Behold, I go forward, but he is not there; and backward, but I cannot perceive him: on the left hand, when he doth work, but I cannot behold him: he hideth himself on the right hand, that I cannot see him." And we are likely to return from all our scientific excursions into the world of nature and of history, to say again with Job: "Lo, these are but the outskirts of his ways: and how small a whisper do we hear of him!"

The precise difficulty felt in all such cases may be, perhaps, thus formulated: Though, by hypothesis, God is the one realest of all facts and the most loving of all beings, he does not seem to be thrust upon us as such at all.

After all is said, is this not the real and great difficulty for the Christian view? And for the establishment of real conviction, and of joyful spiritual living, does not more depend upon meeting effectively this everywhere underlying doubt of the soul, than upon either repeating in new forms the old arguments, or in elaborating new arguments for the existence of God and the possibility of an ideal view of the world? Do we not need to give this particular aspect of our problem such a careful, detailed, and comprehensive consideration as it seldom receives? Just this is our task.

Can something be done, now, to meet this constant, underlying difficulty of the seeming unreality of the spiritual life, felt at the start, and felt after the Christian view is admitted to be the most reasonable? Can the ground be cleared of misconceptions, mistaken prepossessions, certain fallacies of common speech and thought, unreasonable demands, failures to remember essential conditions in our life problems? Can something be done toward giving a really different point of view, that may make the seeming unreality of the spiritual world less a burden to us? In a word, can we see the reasons for the seeming unreality of the spiritual life?

III

THE ORDER OF THE DISCUSSION

Exactly this is the problem of the first of the two large divisions of our inquiry. From the discussion of the reasons for the seeming unreality, we are then to turn, in the second division, in the light of the principles brought out in the first division, to a briefer consideration of the positive way to a convincing sense of reality in religious thought and life. The question is throughout both a theoretical one—of the possible full defense of the theistic view of the world, and a practical one—of the religious life.

From the beginning it seems clear that the reasons for the seeming unreality of the spiritual life would naturally include two classes of causes: those causes which are removable by us; and those causes which lie in the nature of the facts involved, and which while not removable by us, can be recognized and taken into account. That is, there are removable causes, and causes not removable but recognizable.

On the one hand, then, there is the unreality

which is not due to the necessity of the facts, but to something removable in ourselves—the unreality that exists either because certain misconceptions are held which prevent our seeing the problem aright, or because certain conditions are not fulfilled, upon which alone the clearer vision could come. The removable causes, then, are misconceptions of the facts, and failure to fulfil the natural conditions of the spiritual life.

On the other hand, there are the causes which we cannot remove, but which we can recognize: the seeming unreality which is due to the inevitable limitations and fluctuations of our finite natures; and the seeming unreality which is needed for our moral training. While these causes cannot be removed, the clear recognition of them would do, perhaps, most of all to lift the burden of the sense of the unreality of the spiritual world.

We are to turn first, then, to the removable causes

At bottom, both of the removable causes of the seeming unreality of the spiritual life—misconceptions, and failure to fulfil needed conditions—grow out of the deeper failure rightly to relate the spiritual life to the rest of life, to see both its likeness and its difference.

For, it is to be carefully noted, a thing may be unreal to us either because it seems to have no living connection with the rest of our life, or because it seems to have no special contribution to make to life. Some will feel one difficulty most, others the other; but all of us probably feel both difficulties in some degree. So, if the spiritual life is to have reality for us, on the one hand, it must be seen to be of a piece with all life, bound up with the indubitably real world; and yet, on the other hand, it must have individuality—its own reason for being—in its unique and valuable point of view and contribution. That is, the spiritual life must have the reality of connection with all other reals, and the reality of individuality in its own specific contribution to the meaning of life. It must not be so different that it cannot be believed to belong to the same world, and to the same human nature, and to the same God, as the rest of life; and yet it must be seen to be different enough to have a genuine and indispensable contribution of its own to make.

The radical liberal—if I may so call him— feels most the first difficulty, and everywhere has done most to solve it. What Pfleiderer calls the "abstract supernatural" is to this radical liberal a perpetual stumbling-block, and he is ever pointing out the connection, the likeness, and the unity of things. The immanence of God is his one great insistence. The radical orthodox—as perhaps the other temperament may be called—feels most the other difficulty, and has done most for its solution. His great insistence is the transcendence of God. The liberal has done most to establish the likeness; the orthodox, the individuality of religion. And yet, for a man who is willing to see the whole problem, both difficulties are equally real; both solutions are needed; they cannot be thought of as antagonistic. Both the misconceptions of the spiritual life, therefore, and the failure to fulfil its natural conditions, may come from ignoring either the likeness or the difference of the spiritual life.

The two classes of misconceptions of the spiritual life which so arise are particularly plain. Men stumble at the spiritual life, that is, either because it seems so unlike the rest of their life, its conditions all so different; or because they do not see that it has anything of indispensable value to give.

Sometimes the solution of the difficulty of unlikeness seems to have proved too much. It has made religion so like all the rest of life, that religion itself seems to have disappeared in the process. Thus arises the frequent barrenness of the liberal defense of religion. On the other hand, one may seem to make religion so unique as to make it unbelievable, an absolute miracle, with no possible tie of connection with the world we know—an error into which the Ritschlian seems sometimes likely to fall. We shall be guarded against these opposite errors, only by recognizing frankly and fully both needs from the start.

We begin, then, with the misconceptions which come from ignoring the likeness of the spiritual life to the rest of life—its close-knit connections with the whole of existence.

If the spiritual life is a reality at all, we must expect to find it so closely connected with the rest of our life that conditions which hold in all the other realms of our experience will not be without their effect in the spiritual realm. We may not safely forget or ignore, therefore, in the religious life, those great common conditions of all our living which are always at work. Much of our disappointment in spiritual things comes either from quietly ignoring circumstances which we constantly take into account as matters of course in other spheres of life; or from carrying over

2

into the religious life without question certain common fallacies or unwarranted assumptions of ordinary crude thinking, which are felt to be necessarily unspiritual in their implications. Against both mistakes, we have to emphasize the likeness of all the spheres of life: to see, on the one hand, that the spiritual life cannot be set free from the conditions involved in its connection with the rest of life; and, on the other hand, that the fundamental implications of the other spheres of life are not anti-spiritual, as common and cruder views often tacitly assume.

And, first, we need to take into account the effects of the great common conditions of all our living—bodily and psyschical.

PART I

THE CAUSES OF THE SEEMING UNREALITY

MISCONCEPTIONS

IV

IGNORING BODILY CONDITIONS

We find ourselves living an apparently dual life, with its bodily and psychical sides. As to both, we have a certain constitution, the nature and laws of which we may not wisely ignore anywhere. We can regard the constitution of our being and its laws, if we will, as hindrances to be fought against; and the religious life seems often so to have viewed the matter. But it ought not to require much thinking to see that such a course is not only suicidal, but particularly for a thorough-going theistic view, is utterly self-contradictory; for the theistic view must recognize in the nature of men an expression of the will of God himself. The religious life, peculiarly, therefore, is driven to see in the laws of man's being—what scientific discovery and invention see in the laws of nature—not limitations, but the possibility of constantly extending power. Let us make it unmistakably clear to ourselves, then, that it is not beneath the dignity of the spiritual life thoroughly to learn the lesson of modern science: that no conditions are trivial, and that none may be safely ignored.

This certainly means, in the first place, that for the present world, at least, the spiritual life has its bodily conditions. It cannot blindly ignore them, without itself inviting into its heart the sense of unreality. This is to be said neither boastingly nor cynically. It is to be faced as a simple fact. We have bodies, and we cannot set ourselves free from them. As I have elsewhere said,[1]

The long sad history of asceticism in all lands shows how real the religious life has felt this connection with the body to be, and at the same time how fiercely it has resented it. Men have remained, in this question of asceticism, quite too largely on the mythological plane, without any clear sense of a real nature and unity of things. The scientific spirit, which demands a careful study of detailed connections and conditions, has had little enough to do with this blind, fierce struggle; and, in consequence, the ascetic has everywhere, on the one hand, failed to take any sensible account of the effects of ordinary bodily conditions; and, on the other hand, paradoxically enough, has exalted the effects of certain abnormal bodily conditions into higher spiritual attainments. These historical

[1] *Rational Living*, pp. 47-49.

results of religious asceticism certainly cannot be held to commend the method of ignoring bodily conditions. The plain lesson of modern science here would seem to be, that, if the spirit is ever to master the body, it must know its laws and take account of its conditions; these are the very instruments of its mastery. So, and only so, has science made nature serve it.

One can quite understand the reluctance of the spiritual life to admit the closeness of its connection with the physical. It seems itself to be lowered thereby. But it gets no freedom and power by vehemently denying the fact, and ignoring the resulting conditions. Rather, its superiority must be shown, its freedom and power declared, as has been implied, by patient study of the laws of this body and of its connection with the spirit, and by steady fulfilment of the conditions by which alone mastery can come. It is a false and abstract spiritualism, therefore, that hesitates clearly to recognize or to affirm the bodily conditions of the spiritual life. Let us frankly admit that much of the dissatisfaction of the moral and spiritual life results from a wholly unnecessary and senseless disregard of bodily conditions. The emphasis of modern psychology upon the close connection of body and mind, thus, compels the thoughtful man to a study of the bodily conditions of true living.

The man, thus, who means to be saved from

misconception of the spiritual life through ignoring its bodily conditions must bear in mind,
for example, the need of well oxygenated blood,
and the special need of surplus nervous energy
as a chief physical condition of self-control. He
will not forget here, then, the inevitable effect
of fatigue on attention, and consequently upon
self-control. Nor will he forget the close
connection of muscular activity and will, nor
the physical basis of habit. And, on the other
hand, he will recognize the influence of the
mind over the body, and especially the power
of the will in determining conditions of health,
in achieving rest, in avoiding hurry, and in
meeting the special conditions of surplus nervous energy. He will remember, as well, the
physiological effects of faith, and the possible
great liberating force of religion in setting
free the powers of man.

V

FORGETTING THE COMPLEXITY AND UNITY
OF LIFE

When we turn to the misconceptions which
come from ignoring the psychical conditions,
which are common to the whole of life, we
can perhaps deal with them most promptly
and comprehensively by noting the bearing of
what I have called the four great inferences
from modern psychology: the complexity of
life, the unity of the mind, the central importance of will and action, and the concreteness of the real.[1]

And, first, the spiritual life must suffer from
any ignoring of the complexity of life. It is
perhaps not too much to say that the growing
conviction of this complexity of life has changed
our feeling throughout concerning both religion and theology. Their problems do not
seem to us so simple as before, and we are
inclined, therefore, to be less dogmatic, and
at the same time more true to facts. In theology, as well as in psychology, there is taking
place what Professor James has called "the

[1] Treated at length in my *Rational Living*.

reinstatement of the vague and inarticulate to its proper place in our mental life." This makes for truth at the same time that it disturbs dogmatists; and it contains, as well, the key to many of our difficulties which really come from forgetting this intricate complexity of life.

The conviction of the complexity of life brings home, too, to the religious consciousness a fresh sense of the impossibility of the spirit of exclusiveness in the spiritual life. It sees with increasing clearness that there can be no separation of the sacred and secular; that all of life is bound up together. Too often, in their inquiry after the spiritual life, men seem to have been hunting for it as an isolated something, just as the psychologists, as Höffding says, have looked for the *Ego* "as something absolutely simple, which consequently might be given in a certain definite state, in a certain definite sensation or idea." "Hume," he says, "cannot see the trees for the wood." The spiritual life could be presented to us as nothing real in that sense. For that which is an abstract, single, and isolated thing, that which is fundamentally out of relation to all else, becomes thereby a cipher, non-existent and without meaning. What reality could it have?

We shall therefore look for religion not as something apart from life, but in the very midst of it, knit up with the cell and with sex, with all human relations and employments and tendencies and strivings,—inextricably involved in all. And we shall look for its glory not in a majestic isolation, but rather in its ability to permeate and dominate all life. Does not a religion that claims to possess a water-tight compartment of its own thereby proclaim its own impotence and falsity? Is the claim itself not of the very essence of hypocrisy?

From this point of view, there might be real truth in what has seemed to us often the purely pagan exaltation of life-processes, and in the modern psychological explanations (like those of Professor Leuba for example) of many mystical experiences, that do not at the same time deny all value to these experiences. As Professor Davenport puts it, "the human love-passion and the spiritual love-passion appear to modern psychology to be delicately interwoven, particularly in the case of young people between fourteen and twenty-five." Perhaps we have no stronger illustration than just this of the modern recognition of the complexity of life in its bearing on religion.

If this psychological point of view is correct, it will at once be seen that it is an essential misconception of the facts to doubt the reality of the spiritual life because we do not find it as an isolated bit. We could not wish so to find it, if we desired it to be an important factor in life at all. A current illustration may be found in this comment of the *Independent* upon a striking utterance of the distinguished missionary, Dr. Timothy Richard:

"The point of Dr. Richard's argument is this: That if endeavors after conversion are meant merely to cover the strivings to renew men's hearts devotionally without striving to improve men materially, intellectually and nationally, it would seem that only a small part of the kingdom of God makes headway. It is a fact that 'conversion in regard to material, intellectual, social, national and international, as well as devotional aspects, is a conversion towards the establishment of the kingdom of God on earth.'"

In the same way, the spiritual life is certain to suffer from *ignoring the unity of the mind*. For this unity will mean, even more clearly than did the complexity of life, that it will be impossible for us to separate religious experience from the rest of our living. It will mean, further, that there will be plain intellectual, emotional, and volitional conditions[1] of the spiritual life that must be recognized and fulfilled. And just so far as these conditions are not fulfilled, the spiritual life is bound to suffer. And where this is the case, one need not look further for the solution of his religious difficulties.

[1] Cf. *Rational Living*, pp. 111 ff.

VI

KNOWLEDGE NEVER MERELY PASSIVE

In the same way, no rational conception of the spiritual life can afford to forget the modern psychological emphasis upon the central importance of will and action. This conviction will plainly affect the entire point of view, and may easily change, as we shall see, what have come to seem commonplaces in religious thinking and living. A misconception, that is, of the psychological facts here must inevitably affect our spiritual insight and the success of our spiritual living.

In particular, the psychological emphasis on the central importance of will and action means that religious thinking must not forget the practical nature of all knowledge and belief.

Certainly this principle means that knowledge is never a merely passive process, as probably it is commonly conceived. It involves at every stage the creative activity of the mind. In the most passive experience conceivable, the mind itself has something to contribute. A purely passive impression is a psychological abstraction, never an actual fact. In no case, whether in our relation to the world of the senses, or in our relation to other minds, or in our relation to God, can there be any literal transfer of thought or feeling. We get partial data only, which we complete and then interpret. In even the closest personal intercourse, it is worth noticing, the words spoken are, after all, only signs of ideas that must be created on both sides. Even the receiving mind must actively create the ideas, suggested by the words spoken by the other, in view of its own entire experience. There is no possible way, in even the directest knowledge, of getting rid of this interpretation of given data, out of experience. The conditions of religious knowledge, therefore, are in no way unique in this respect. The principle has its immediate bearing upon the reality of prayer, and of inspiration, and of revelation from God. For it requires that there should always be a human interpretive element in all these experiences.

A chief difficulty, for example, in prayer is no doubt found for many in the lack of a felt presence, and the lack of a definite response, such as the person feels that he gets in his relation to the outer world, or to another

person. As to this difficulty it might be said
at once, as Hinton suggests, that all the final
forces, even in external nature, are unseen and
not as they seem to us. The constant pressure
of the air, the motion of the earth, we do not
feel at all. We have no sensible knowledge,
of any kind, of the existence or nature of atoms.
The ether vibrations are quite beyond the reach
of any sense.

But the principle which we are here considering—that knowledge is never merely passive—contains a more adequate answer to the
difficulty. There is really a very close analogy
between the knowledge of the outer world,
which we gain through sensations, and the
knowledge of the spiritual world which comes
from the data of our inner life. In neither
case can it be said that there are immediate
knowledge and revelation. In both, what we
call our immediate knowledge has been a long
time building, and has involved not only the
first impressions, but comparison, memory, and
reasoning. In neither case is a literal transfer
of full-fledged thought or knowledge possible.
God's revelation of himself cannot be a literal
transfer of a message as by a written note; and
even if there were literal words spoken or
written, they would still require interpreta-

tion, and be capable of very different meanings, as interpreted out of different experiences.

Lotze, in a thoughtful passage in his *Microcosmus,* brings out carefully this comparison between our relation to the world of sense and to the world of spirit:[1]

"Every sensuous impression regarded in itself is but a way in which we are affected, some phase of our own condition; in itself it gives no knowledge of any matter of fact, taken alone it constitutes no experience. Here again it is only our thought which, mastering the manifold revelations of sense, compares and combines them, or interprets given combinations, thus arriving through them at the knowledge of some fact. We can hardly picture to ourselves the workings of God upon the heart otherwise than after this pattern; we cannot imagine the recognition of any fact as something that can be simply communicated, something that reaches the mind ready-made and without any activity on its part; we can only imagine that occasion can be given to the mind to, as it were, produce such recognition by exercising this activity, and in this it is that every appropriation of a truth must consist. As sense in itself furnishes merely an

[1] Vol. II, p. 662.

impression, so also this divine influence would produce merely a feeling, a mood, a mode of affection; what is thus experienced becomes a revelation only through some work of reflection which analyzes its content and reduces it to coherence by clear notions that are capable of being combined with our ideas of the real world."

That we have these inner data, as a sufficient and legitimate basis for our gradually developing knowledge of the spiritual world, it is hardly open to any thoughtful observer of the ways of his own spirit to question. Doubtless God's response in our spiritual life is not made without our own active coöperation; but he does answer, and we have had that answer in a thousand different quickenings, glimpses, times of conviction, and "sober and strenuous moods". The really needed guidance and coöperation of God must be constant, rather than here and there by some marked interference; and his answer to us, therefore, in the life of prayer is not merely at the time of our prayer, or through consciously definite leadings. Rather is he always at work with us; and the justification of our faith is, that in the long retrospect there is plain growth in this inner life, increasing assurance of the spiritual, and that our relation to God is coming to mean more and more as we go on.

VII

NO MERELY THEORETICAL SOLUTIONS

All our knowing, then, once more is necessarily bound up with the whole man and with the whole of life. And this must mean that in religion, certainly, no merely theoretical solution of our problem is possible. Everything that has been said in recent psychological literature as to the importance of action and of the practical interests, particularly in their relation to the solution of all our ultimate problems, shows this.[1] If, in body and in mind alike, we are made for action, if we ourselves are prevailingly practical, it need not seem so strange that our solutions of ultimate questions must depend perhaps mainly on practical considerations. And if we are made for action, it is most fitting, moreover, that those convictions, which are to give support to action, should themselves be wrought out in action. The principle of the laboratory method would be justified here most of all. "In truth, when one thinks deeply enough about it, he must see, further, that for the most fundamental

[1] Cf. King: *Rational Living*, pp. 154 ff.

problems no other than a practical solution is possible in the nature of the case. There can be no mere theoretical proof or disproof of the trustworthiness of our faculties, for example. One could only use the very faculties in question in such a proof. The only proof possible is the practical power to use them."[1]

To these more fundamental considerations it may be worth while to add a number of brief suggestions that naturally connect themselves with this discussion of the practical nature of our knowledge, and that meet certain common difficulties of faith.

Mathematics has been so often extolled as the ideal of reasoning, and is so commonly held to be a peculiarly good training for the reasoning powers, that it is well worth insisting that there is no such thing as mathematical demonstration possible in the world of concrete realities. Indeed, the mathematician, on the contrary, is likely to be a particularly poor reasoner in practical matters, if he allows his mathematical point of view to dominate, just because his prevailing habit of thought is abstract. Demonstration is possible, even in mathematics, only because the mind itself makes the concepts with which it deals; they

[1] King: *Rational Living*, pp. 165-166.

are abstracts, capable of definition in a finite number of terms. In every sphere of actual life, on the other hand, we are shut up to concretes that cannot be so defined, and therefore are limited to probable reasoning. To ask for overwhelming evidence in the sense of demonstration in the spiritual life, then, is to ask for that which never can be given us in any realm of the concrete.

Sometimes the demand for "overwhelming evidence" in the spiritual life means that one wishes the conviction that comes from personal experience, before fulfilling the conditions upon which alone that experience can come. It seems to be true that we come into all the higher experiences of life in one of two ways:[1] either the necessary course of our lives thrusts the experience upon us, and though we did not choose it and would not have chosen it, we find the actual experience meaning to us what we could not have guessed beforehand, and then choose it for its own sake; or, we have to make the venture with a kind of desperate faith that the experience will be to us what others have found it, for the highest things everywhere require the complete commitment,— they give themselves only where all is risked.

[1] Cf. King: *Personal and Ideal Elements in Education*, pp. 151 ff.

No temporizing, half-hearted experiment here will give results. The meaning of a genuinely unselfish love, for example, does not yield itself to any calculating experiment. Either one is surprised into it, or he must voluntarily venture all in complete self-abandonment, burning all his bridges behind him. It should be no surprise to us, therefore, that in the highest sphere of value, that of religion, with its pre-eminently ethical and personal emphasis, there should be no way of getting the conviction of individual experience before experience. There are, then, two temperaments, and two ways of coming into the great values of life; but there is no way of avoiding the need of experience.

A closely related suggestion needs also to be heeded if we are really to recognize how impossible a merely theoretical solution is in religion; though here, too, religion makes no peculiar demand. Throughout life we are continually encountering experiences of which we instinctively realize that it is useless to speak, except to those who have had a like experience. It is useless to talk of color to a man born blind, or of beauty to a man who never had the living emotion of the beautiful. Our words in all such cases are only the names for experiences; they cannot disclose the ex-

periences themselves. The very meaning of
the words here is not chiefly a thought product
at all. We have lived the meaning, and know
it only so far as we have lived it. After all,
the one great teacher is life, and our best words
to another of even the deepest in us must fall
resultless, until life has brought to the other
the experience out of which the words can be
interpreted. We can only bear witness. How
impossible, then, is it by any logical means to
bring home the full reality of the spiritual
world, where the conditions of the possible
experience are not fulfilled! In Whitman's
putting:

> "No one can acquire for another—not one,
> No one can grow for another—not one.
> The song is to the singer, and comes back
>   most to him.
> The teaching is to the teacher, and comes back
>   most to him.
>
>   .   .   .   .   .   .
>
> And no man understands any greatness or
>   goodness but his own, or the indica-
>   tion of his own."

We cannot inherit the sense of reality in the
spiritual world. There is no reality in religion
without a living experience of our own.

So, too, one cannot thoughtfully face the broad facts of human experience without feeling how unreasonable is the seeming expectation, frequently cherished, of ability to meet all the difficulties of the reality of the spiritual world at once and out of hand. The considerations just passed over show how often one must wait for the interpreting power of experience. Moreover, even when our conclusions are really sound, we may be quite unable fully to state the reasons. The grounds of our faith, we have seen, the whole trend of modern psychology shows to be not merely intellectual, but interwoven with a great complex of human interests, only slowly appreciated. The truth is, probably, always greater than our reasons for holding it.

But even if the problem be regarded in a given case as purely intellectual, it must still be remembered that real speculative power is neither very common, nor is it developed early in life. It is peculiarly appropriate, therefore, to suggest to the young that unrest must naturally be the result of a large reading of speculative authors before there have been acquired such mental development and dialectic skill as will enable one to overcome the pressure of the author in hand. Why should one expect, without very wide and special training in these themes, at once and out of hand to meet and settle all the points a subtle mind can raise in a labored work? Is it sensible to suppose that there is no answer to our difficulty, because an answer is not immediately suggested? The universal human interest in these deeper questions involved in the religious life must of course lead to much general thinking; but there seems still dire need of reminding many that men are not born philosophers and born theologians any more than born botanists. However reluctantly, one is simply compelled to recognize sometimes colossal ignorance in this sphere on the part of men otherwise well educated. Let the young, at least, be content to let the philosophers devour one another for the time being, while they go on with their living. One may well remind himself, here, of Augustine Birrell's dictum that "the verdict to be striven for is not 'well-guessed', but 'well-done.'"

Again, many seem to think it incumbent upon them, when overtaken by doubts in the religious life, to begin their inquiry as if the questions were wholly new, to be solved by them from the beginning; although they would hardly dream of taking such a course in other matters. Is it true, indeed, that nothing has been proved so far? Are the history and experience of the centuries to count for nothing? The man, for example, who takes up Christianity to-day, as a new problem, to be solved by him as if Christ had just come, it is manifest, deliberately throws away a very large factor in the solution of the problem.

It is a perfectly legitimate use of the appeal to consequences which Newman Smyth makes, when he urges, "Not growing discord, which betrays a method which is wrong, but growing peace, which shows that the method of life is right, is the world's experience of Christianity." This broader appeal to what the consequences are in the long run—like the scientific verifying of an hypothesis by appeal to experience—is rightly insisted upon in present-day philosophy, and can be logically set aside only by one, who is willing to deny the fundamental assumption of our thinking,— that we are dealing with an honest world. "For," as Professor Seth Pattison contends,[1] "the *ultima ratio* of every creed, the *ultima ratio* of truth itself, is that it *works;* and no greater condemnation can be passed upon a doctrine or system than that, if it were true,

[1] *Man's Place in the Cosmos,* p. 307.

human life, as it has been lived by the best of the race, would cease to be reasonable, or rather, would become a phenomenon whose emergence it was impossible to explain."

Mr. Shorthouse, in his *Spiritual Romance of John Inglesant,* has made his seeker after truth reach this final conclusion: "We find ourselves immersed in physical and psychological laws, in accordance with which we act, or from which we diverge. Whether we are free to act or not, we can at least fancy we resolve. Let us cheat ourselves, if it be a cheat, with this fancy, for we shall find that by so doing we actually attain the end we seek. . . . . We shall find man has attained any position of vantage he may occupy by following the laws, which our instinct and conscience tell us are Divine." The argument is a good one against the confirmed and persistent doubter. But on what possible scheme of thought, pray, can that freedom, and those laws, by means of which it is granted we obtain whatever of value life possesses, be regarded as "cheats"? It is pure illusion to talk of proofs at all, if freedom were not so proved. The healthful mind cannot be brought to believe in any such hideous discord in the nature of things. Augustine Birrell speaks of sentimental sceptics "who, after laboring to demolish

what they call the chimera of superstition, fall
to weeping as they remember they have now
no lies to teach their children."

In any case, it is particularly true in the
matter of the religious life, that the questions
are not new. Entirely decisive and universally
convincing answers, doubtless, we are still unable to give; but, even if no reasons can be
suggested why our answers are not more decisive, we may at least recognize that the
difficulties, also, are not essentially new. We
need to learn the calm and patience of history.
No generation has had to face a greater intellectual revolution than our own; and yet it
cannot be honestly said that the religious questions and difficulties of our time are greatly
different in their essence from those of other
days. The contrary assumption is often made,
and proves a real hindrance; but we have a
right to urge, particularly with the young, that
the way to a reasonable religious faith is not
more difficult now than at any previous time,
but rather is in all probability easier than ever,
as it ought to be, if men are profiting at all
by the experience of the past.

Psychology's rightful recognition of the practical and of the whole man, may remind us
again that, in finding our way into satisfactory

religious living and thinking, there is real danger of over-rating intellectual difficulties and particularly merely negative criticism. A single difficulty is sometimes made the end of all faith. But we may be sure that no single difficulty, like that of the relativity of human knowledge, for example, easily phrased and still more easily misapplied, sums up all of philosophy or of life, or furnishes reason for forthwith setting aside all hitherto held as true. The great broad teaching of human life and experience may not be so easily nullified. We need not be in haste. There is particular danger here for those of the preëminently practical temperament, and especially where strong desire or passion is involved. As soon as the full reason for a hitherto trusted moral or religious principle is not immediately forthcoming, the desire, held in leash by the principle, is given full rein. I think it was Clerk Maxwell, who wrote in a private letter, after various intellectual excursions of this kind: "Old Chap! I have read up many queer religions; there is nothing like the old thing after all. I have looked into most philosophical systems, and I have seen that none will work without a God." It is easy to overestimate the difficulties.

An incidental suggestion of Lotze's may well be added here. "We are accustomed," he says, "to estimate one and the same idea very differently when it comes before us as a conjecture, and when it is offered as the expression of a fact."[1] We may scout a view as utterly preposterous and unthinkable beforehand, that, as a proved fact, we later find wholly reasonable, and assimilate with entire equanimity. Let one think, for example, of the fact of alternate generation among some of the lower animals, and of the now undoubted parthenogenesis of the drone bees. So, in much of our thinking, especially along the lines of ultimate philosophical and religious inquiry, quite too great weight may be easily given to *a priori* objections.

And it needs also clearly to be recognized that we can nowhere rest in merely negative criticism. A quite unreasonable importance, it is certain, has been accorded in theistic argument to this kind of criticism. What Professor Bowne says so vigorously of philosophical scepticism holds of all merely negative criticism: "The sceptic acquires importance, not through the doubts he utters, but through those which he rationally justifies. The judicial critic,

[1] *Microcosmus,* Vol. II, p. 140.

therefore, must compel the sceptic to take his place along with other theorists, and give reasons for the unfaith that is in him. Until he does this, his position is arbitrary, capricious, and irrational. Strangely enough, this manifest dictate of logic has often been overlooked in the history of speculation; and dogmatic denial, especially if it be of some important practical interest, has been judged to have high speculative significance. The ease with which good people have been stampeded by unsupported denial is one of the humorous features of the history of philosophy."[1] The serious thinker, says Seth Pattison, "will always repeat the words of Kant, that in itself doubt is not a permanent resting place for human reason. Its justification is relative, and its function transitional."[2]

Once more, in considering the psychological conditions of the sense of reality in the spiritual life, we may not forget the natural results that come from a long ignoring of facts. Here, too, the religious life is not at all peculiar. The law is one common to all the spheres of our living. Our entire consciousness is characterized, the psychologists tell us, by a constant selective

[1] *Theory of Thought and Knowledge*, p. 269.
[2] *Encyclopaedia Britannica*.   Article, Scepticism.

4

activity. To certain elements in our environment we attend; certain others we persistently ignore. These ignored elements practically drop out of our life; they have for us no real existence. For all practical purposes, they have ceased to be. So too, no doubt, the seeming unreality of the spiritual world in the case of many is due, in no small degree, to the long ignoring of the facts of the spiritual world in their previous lives and habits of thought. "We hear much," writes Professor Peabody, "of the reasons which lead men to abandon prayer, but in most such instances the loss of the prayer habit does not happen because of profound philosophizing or serious conviction, but through sheer inertia. There are so many other things to do, that, as a young man once said, 'One does not get around to his prayers!' "[1]

The fact of the existence of God, as he is revealed to us in Christ, is no barren truth. The rational inferences to be drawn from it will bear on every detail of life. But here is a man, perhaps, (I am very far from believing that this is a universal explanation) into whose life for years no conscious recognition of God and the spiritual life has come; who has acted precisely as if they were not; who has thus

[1] *Mornings in the College Chapel. Second Series,* p. 9.

virtually denied their existence in every act; whose thoughts, plans, purposes, have been all apart from God; who has settled habits of thought and life, that are logically consistent only with denial of the existence of God and a spiritual life. Will those habits have no influence on his spiritual insight? Is he to come now, at one bound, into the clear and simple vision of God and divine truth, which may have belonged to his childhood? And shall he refuse to have patience to take the toilsome way back to those early convictions from which his lack of earnestness, his carelessness, his indifference, his neglect, his worldliness, and his sin have separated him? Verily, I sometimes think, it were a strange thing, if the spiritual life were not obscure to many of us. If the voice within us were not indeed divine, long since would it have been smothered under the heaped up rubbish of the years.

VIII

THE PRACTICAL NATURE OF ALL BELIEF

But the psychological emphasis upon the influence of the practical interests in all consciousness, and upon the whole concrete life of the whole man, not only means—as we have been seeing—that in the knowledge of the spiritual we may not ignore these conditions of all knowledge, but also particularly means that we are not to forget the practical nature of all belief.

That I may not simply repeat a line of thought which I have elsewhere given[1] let me substitute bodily Professor Bowne's very clear and suggestive statement upon this point: "The sum is this: The mind is not a disinterested logic machine, but a living organism, with manifold interests and tendencies. These outline its development, and furnish the driving power. The implicit aim in mental development is to recognize these interests, and make room for them, so that each shall have its proper field and object. In this way a series

[1] *Cf. Theology and the Social Consciousness*, pp. 78-81. *Rational Living*, pp. 161 ff.

of ideals arise in our mental life. As cognitive, we assume that the universe is rational. Many of its elements are opaque, and utterly unmanageable by us at present, but we assume spontaneously and unconsciously that at the center all is order, and that there all is crystalline and transparent to intelligence. Thus there arises in our thought the conception of a system in which all is light, a system whose foundations are laid in harmony, and whose structure is rational law, a system every part of which is produced and maintained and illumined by the majestic and eternal Reason. But this is only a cognitive ideal, to which experience yields but little support. But we hold fast the ideal and set aside the facts which make against it as something not yet comprehended."

"But we are moral beings also, and our moral interests must be recognized. Hence arises a moral ideal, which we join to the cognitive. The universe must be not only rational, but righteous at its root. Here too we set aside the facts which make against our faith as something not yet understood. This is especially the case in dealing with the problem of evil. Here we are never content with finding a cause for the good and evil in experience; we insist upon an explanation which shall save the assumed goodness at the heart of things."

"Finally, we are religious, and our entire nature works together to construct the religious ideal. The intellect brings its ideal; and the conscience brings its ideal; and the affections bring their ideal; and these, together with whatever other thought of perfection we may have, are united into the thought of the one Perfect Being, the ideal of ideals, the supreme and complete, to whom heart, will, conscience, and intellect alike may come and say, 'Thy Kingdom come; thy will be done.' Here, as in the previous cases, we do not ignore the facts which make against the view, but we set them aside as things to be explained, but which must not in any way be allowed to weaken our faith."

"All of these ideals are, primarily, alike subjective. They are produced, indeed, under the stress of experience, but they are not transcripts of any possible experience. That transparent universe of the reason is as purely a mental product as that righteous universe of the conscience, or as the supreme perfection of religion. In each of these cases the mind appears with its subjective ideals, and demands that reality shall recognize them; and in all

alike reality recognizes them only imperfectly.
To some extent the universe is intelligible. To
some extent the power not ourselves makes for
righteousness. To some extent God is revealed.
But in all these cases a purely logical and objective contemplation of the known facts would
leave us in great uncertainty. The assured conviction we have rests upon no logical deduction
from experience, but upon the optimistic assumption that the mind has a right to itself,
and is at home in the universe. The mind will
not consent to abandon its nature and resign
itself to utter mental and moral confusion. This
is, to be sure, an act of pure faith, but it is an
act upon which our entire mental life depends.
A purely speculative knowledge of reality,
which shall be strictly deductive and free from
assumption, is impossible."[1]

The spiritual life—the religious view—then,
let it be clearly seen, makes here no peculiar
demand. It stands side by side with other
ideals, having a like original justification. That
it must take account of practical and ideal
interests is in no way peculiar to it; but of
these practical and ideal interests it must take
account. Not to do so, is to end in hopeless
confusion, not in greater clearness.

[1] *Philosophy of Theism*, pp. 19-22.

IX

SOME COMMON LOGICAL FALLACIES

This practical nature of all belief itself indicates that, for the sake of the spiritual life itself, a protest is constantly needed in the interests of the *whole concrete reality and of the whole man*. In the last analysis, perhaps the greatest danger that can beset a man's spiritual life and thought is to misconceive both as having to do only with some fraction of a man's being or living. As to our religious thinking, this means that we are to avoid the mistakes which come from forgetting the influence of certain common logical fallacies, and the mistake of failing to set aside certain traditional objections, which are supposed to put religious faith and life at peculiar disadvantage.

And, first, let us be sure that the spiritual life is guarded from the influence of certain logical fallacies which, while very common, are none the less unwarranted and dangerous. Nowhere more than in our ultimate thinking upon spiritual themes do we need to be sure of the soundness of our reasoning. Two of these common fallacies have been already implied in the emphasis upon the practical nature of all knowledge and belief, and may be merely mentioned in this summary view of such logical mistakes, namely: the two great and far reaching mistakes of ignoring all that cannot be precisely formulated, and so yielding to the constant temptation to cut short the facts to suit our theories; and, particularly, of making the intellectual the sole standard of reality, and so practically identifying the logical and the metaphysical. The history of philosophy and the history of theology teem with examples of both mistakes, some of which have been already noted.

Besides these, three other common fallacies deserve attention: those of being dominated by a word, by an analogy, and by what is imageable. In all these cases the fundamental difficulty is that the word or the analogy or the image is not really thought through.

One would hardly believe, were the evidence not forced upon him, the extent to which the thought of even professional thinkers has been *dominated by words*. The only deliverance from such domination is the persistent determination to use no words without having some clear corresponding thought. Domination by a word whose implications are never made really clear, it has been often noted, is seen in the constant use, by Locke and his followers, of the word "impression." No doubt an inadequate analogy is also strongly at work here. Taken together, the domination has been so real, that "the tang of Locke's cask," as some one has expressed it, is to be recognized in very much of English thought down to the present.

Domination by a word is particularly easy, when the word has a double meaning, or seems capable, at least, of looking in two directions at once. Thus, many have hidden from themselves the real difficulties of their conception by the choice of the word "impulse"; which has both a recognized physical and psychical meaning, and so seems admirably adapted to serve as an explanatory principle, that shall be neither a mechanical force nor a conscious mind. These people seem never to have compelled themselves to face the question, whether they could really think any *tertium quid,* corresponding to the ambiguity of the word. There has been a similar playing with the word "appearance," the word "thought," and the word "force." And—not to extend enumeration of examples—it particularly concerns the thinker on religious themes to notice, that one may be successfully challenged to give any clear meaning to the term "impersonal spirit," and to similar designations, that have nowhere figured more largely than in anti-theistic discussions. We are not to be bullied by a word, however sonorous or often repeated. We may and we must demand, if we have any desire really to reach the truth, that every term have a clear corresponding thought. It is not vain to insist upon the point. Over and over again in the history of thought, great interests have been sacrificed to a word.

The extent to which men are satisfied, in their search for an explanation, by mere names, is another almost humorous illustration of this domination by words. Few seem to have made it clear to themselves, for example, that naming a comparatively unknown force is no explanation of it, or that a "law" of nature is no explanation of the why and wherefore of the phenomena whose behavior the law only formulates.

Domination by a striking *analogy* is still more common and more dangerous. It is more dangerous because the analogy may be supposed to be partly applicable. The mind then accepts it as wholly adequate, instead of insisting on a clear recognition of the precise limitations of the analogy. It then substitutes for real thinking upon the subject in hand, the much easier process of drawing out the analogy. It may even congratulate itself upon some peculiarly deep thinking, when it has abused its analogy, in making it "go on all fours." One can hardly doubt, for example, that theology has often so abused the analogy of human law and government. And it is worth serious thought by us all, just now, whether under the stimulus of the idea of evolution, with its manifold applications, we are not all in danger of unthinking domination by the biological analogy. Let us say frankly, that much of this biological thinking on spiritual themes is simply not thinking at all, but just deluding ourselves with a half-thought analogy. And let us recall Lotze's protest—when the world was once before going wild over a precisely similar idea— against the term *organic,* "for which," he says, "a long defense will have to be made if at the last day account has to be given for every idle word."[1]

Once more, we are peculiarly liable to delusion, when a matter can be in some way presented to us in an *image,* although we may not be able truly to think it at all. The clearness

[1] *Microcosmus,* Vol. II, p. 183.

and apparent obviousness of the image of an
actual contact or impact of two bodies, for example, is felt, probably, by most to solve forthwith the whole problem of the possibility of
reciprocal action; although, in truth, it throws
not a particle of light upon the difficult question of how we are really to *think* the reciprocal
action as taking place. And so in countless
problems, the mere imaging power is made
to take the place of thinking; and it does it so
effectively, that often the really serious difficulties are not even raised. Almost all the force
of much anti-theistic argument lies in this
shallow appeal to the power of sense-imagery.
The argument seems to get on swimmingly
because it moves on a crude sense plane, and
never faces the real difficulties, which require
a final theistic view for their solution. The difficult problem of interaction, already referred
to, is a good example of such ignored difficulties.
So, too, by imaging laws to themselves as some
kind of real existences, men seem to be able to
accomplish much without needing to assume
God, and escape many difficult questions; but
the process can hardly be called thinking. Such
theorists tell us that, grant them matter, force,
and laws, they will easily show how the cosmos
has arisen from chaos. The appeal here is

almost wholly to the imaging power, and—to mention but a single difficulty—the view quite fails to make clear how that in which laws already rule can be in any sense a "chaos." It is to be regretted that the philosophizing of men whose training has been wholly in natural science, has been so largely on this plane of simple appeal to the sense imagination. Perhaps no one of late has shown more convincingly the weakness of this kind of reasoning than Ward, in his *Naturalism and Agnosticism.*

X

SOME TRADITIONAL OBJECTIONS

Besides the influence of these common fallacies, religious thinking and living are likely to be hindered by failing to set aside certain traditional objections, that are supposed to put religious life and thought at peculiar disadvantage.

Some of these have been already implied, and need only be mentioned here: like the objections that come from an abstract intellectualism, from a crude sensationalism, and from an impossible hypostasizing of laws, and, in general, from a quite unwarrantable exaltation of the mathematico-mechanical view of the world. These are, in fact, simply inherited bugbears. The truth is, as it may be hoped we are more and more coming to see, that all these views, from which objection arises, are themselves so involved in difficulties and self-contradictions that, when an attempt is made clearly to think them through, they are driven to abandon their position of self-sufficiency and to admit that they themselves require an ideal view to complete them. The universal abandonment of materialism is one interesting illustration of this trend.

Besides these objections, already briefly considered, which arise more from the point of view of natural science, there are other objections inherited from the philosophical point of view, which are often supposed to put the religious life at peculiar disadvantage. Without going into elaborate argument upon any one of these points, we can perhaps see that none of them have any such decisive weight against the religious life as has been supposed.

And, first, we ought carefully to observe that there is absolutely no ground for the very common tacit assumption, that the theistic view is in any *peculiar* way bound up with all the difficulties of the problems of the theory of knowledge and of metaphysics. It is rather creditable than otherwise to theistic thinking, that this impression has come to prevail; for it shows, at least, that theistic thinkers generally have tried to be really thorough-going in their inquiries, and to shirk no problems, however difficult, in the attempt to reach a genuinely unified view of the world. And yet, the solving of all the difficult problems of epistemology and metaphysics is, in truth, no responsibility belonging peculiarly to religion. It might be justly urged that the very objects of science indicate that it, rather than religion, should be here specially concerned. The problems are difficult, but the difficulties are philosophical, and they exist for all thinkers alike, and are not only no more difficult for a theistic view than for any other, but seem rather to require some kind of theistic view for their solution. In any case, epistemological and metaphysical difficulties are not at all peculiarly religious difficulties.

So, too, the doctrine of the relativity of human knowledge has been long supposed to make peculiar difficulties for religion. The theory affirms that all human knowledge is relative; we cannot reach absolute truth, but only what is true for us, and this may greatly differ from the absolute truth. All our conceptions of God must be after the constitution of our own minds—"anthropomorphic"—it is said, and therefore untrustworthy. The Infinite God must then be for us essentially unknowable. The sweep of the objection is to be noted. It makes all inquiry useless. The inference from the theory is supposed to be that every evidence of divine truths may be set aside, because however it may seem to us, since our knowledge is merely relative, we cannot have attained anything of value in our inquiry—no real truth.

5

As to the inference from the theory, a few things may be said.

The theory states no new truth. When we say that human knowledge is relative, we only affirm what most of us learned long since, that human knowledge is human knowledge, not angelic or divine, and has consequently human limitations—a doctrine quite as old as Job. We need not then be greatly disconcerted, or driven off the field by large words, "anthropomorphic" or otherwise.

The inference drawn from the theory really denies the trustworthiness of our reason. We suppose that reason has given us some real truths in the religious sphere, and we are told, "Not so; they cannot be relied on, for your thought is relative." This makes all science equally impossible. The first induction of science goes upon the assumption of the truth of our instincts, upon the principle as expressed by a clear thinker,[1] that "the world within us, and the world without us are parts of the same whole, and thus must be related to one another. They must be at heart the same. Thus by the same principle which gives us authority to make the slightest generalization which goes beyond the enumerated facts, we are authorized

[1] C. C. Everett: *The Science of Thought,* p. 375.

to assume that the necessary forms of our thought have some relation definite and real to the forms of existence outside of us."

Upon this point Professor Simon has these forcible words:[1] "Convince man that his thinking must be untrue because it is his, and thinking will be paralyzed; but surely that which paralyzes thought cannot be true for thought. Besides I would reply in the language of Scripture, 'God created man in his own image; in the image of God created he him'—words which the German philosopher Jacobi aptly applied to this subject when he said, 'Man anthropomorphizes in thinking God, because God theomorphized in creating man.' "

It is one thing to say that our knowledge is finite, partial, and quite another to affirm that it is therefore no true knowledge. This illustration has been used: "Could the inanimate worlds conceive of God, from their lower degree of relations, they would conceive of him as the infinite force. This conception would be partial, yet true as far as it went. No higher conception could leave out that of the infinite force. So the plant would, and rightly, conceive of God as the infinite life. That conception would be true, though partial. The spirit con-

[1] *Bibliotheca Sacra,* January '87, p. 4.

ceives of him as the infinite spirit. This is still true, but still partial."

While distinctly less terrifying than it was, this doctrine of the relativity of knowledge still seems to many the sum of wisdom; and the current naturalism makes much of it, in one form or another. It is the very heart of Ward's able discussion of *Naturalism and Agnosticism,* to show that this strange alliance of naturalism and agnosticism is really fatal to naturalism; that really to think through the implication of such common scientific terms as "phenomena" and "law" and "method" is to see that science itself cannot admit, without self-destruction, such a complete and final relativity in human knowledge as agnosticism asserts. In other words, the doctrine of the relativity of human knowledge is terrifying, not because it is a peculiarly deep probing of the problem of the theory of knowledge, but just because it does not go to the bottom. It loses all its terrors as a peculiar difficulty for ideal views as soon as the problem of knowing is vigorously grappled.

Professor Ward's own way of getting at the matter may be seen in a condensed statement from his first chapter. He has summed up the common naturalistic position in two statements.

"These two statements," he goes on to say, "amount to saying, first, that there is no knowledge save scientific knowledge, or knowledge of phenomena and of their relations, and secondly, that this knowledge is non-theistic. It is worth our while to note that in a sense both these propositions are true, and *that* is the sense in which science in its every-day work is concerned with them. But again there is a sense in which, taken together, these propositions are not true, but this is a sense that will only present itself to the critic of knowledge reflecting upon knowledge as a whole. Thus it is true that science has no need, and indeed, can make no use, in any particular instance, of the theistic hypothesis. That hypothesis is specially applicable to nothing just because it claims to be equally applicable to everything. Recourse to it would involve just that discontinuity which it is the cardinal rule of scientific method to avoid. But, because reference to the Deity will not serve for a physical explanation in physics or a chemical explanation in chemistry, it does not therefore follow that the sum total of scientific knowledge is equally intelligible whether we accept the theistic hypothesis or not. Again, it is true that every item of scientific knowledge is concerned with some definite relation of definite phenomena and with nothing else. But, for all that, the systematic organization of such items may quite well yield further knowledge which transcends the special relations of definite phenomena. In fact, so surely as science collectively is more than a mere aggregate of items or 'knowledges,' as Bacon would have said, so surely will the whole be more, and yield more, than the mere sum of its facts."

"In other words," he says later, "ideally complete science will become philosophy. This conceit or doctrine of an absolute boundary between science and nescience and the endeavor to identify with it a like sharp separation between empirical knowledge and philosophic speculation may then, we conclude, be both dismissed as 'sophistical and illusory.' Nevertheless, as I have said, these notions are widely current in one shape or other, save among the few in these days, who have even a passman's acquaintance with the rudiments of epistemology. One of the most plausible and not least prevalent forms of this doctrine is embodied in the shallow Comtian 'Law of Development,' according to which there are three stages in human thought, the theological, the metaphysical, and the positive; the metaphysical superseding the theological and being in turn superseded by the positive or scientific. A glance at the past history of knowledge would show at once the facts that make these views so specious and yet prove them to be false."[1]

So far, then, as it is regarded as peculiarly a difficulty for a theistic view, or as precluding a real relation to God, we may regard this ghost of relativity as quite exorcised for us.

[1] *Naturalism and Agnosticism,* pp. 23-4; 29-30.

XI

DIFFICULTY IN THE CONCEPTION OF GOD

There are, still, certain special applications of the doctrine of relativity that, because of their direct bearing on the religious life, it may be worth while briefly to consider. It is often urged, that the very terms we apply to God show that we must be out of any real living relation to him. The term 'Absolute,' for example, has been made, of itself, to settle the whole matter. The Absolute, it is said, is that which by hypothesis is out of all relations, and with which, therefore, it is of course not possible to come into relations. One would be almost ashamed to call attention to such pure verbal jugglery, if it had not been so often solemnly paraded as an argument of vital consequence. God is not the Absolute, let us unhesitatingly say, as being unrelated. A being out of all relation to all else— incapable, that is, of any possible reciprocal action with other beings—would be as nearly a nonentity as we could well conceive, if indeed it were possible to conceive such a supposed being at all. On the contrary, God is the Absolute rather, in that he is the being in whom all relations find their reason and possibility of existence.

Nor is God the Absolute in the sense that he is without qualities. This would be to assert that he is without content, whereas we must rather conceive of God as having the richest, largest, fullest content, in the direction of Spinoza's idea of an infinite number of attributes. Positively, the Absolute as applied to God ought to mean, raised above all the limitations which pertain to the finite as a mere part of a whole—the final and fundamental source of all, unexhausted in any or all of his manifestations.

Similar statements need to be made about the use of the word *unchangeable,* as applied to God. God is unchangeable in the consistency of the meaning of his nature and of his loving purpose. But instead of this making it true that there can then be no change in him answering to our need, it rather insures such adjusting activity as his love requires. This whole false notion of unchangeableness in God goes back to a metaphysically false and abandoned notion of an ever identical stuff or substance, and should no longer be allowed to obscure our religious thinking or living. We are to believe in a really living God, who is in the realest reciprocal action with all the finite, and with whom, therefore, our inner attitude does make a difference.

And when we have once gotten rid of these spectres of an unthinkable Absolute and of an ever-identical substance, we discover that that other ghost is also laid, that supposes that there is some profound philosophical difficulty in prayer or in any revelation. There is, in truth, no sound reason, philosophical or scientific, for denying that God has actual access to our minds. Lotze certainly did not speak without full knowledge of all the difficulties involved when he said: "There is nothing whatever that stands in opposition to the further conviction that God, at particular moments and in particular persons, may have stood nearer to humanity, or may have revealed himself at such moments and in such persons in a more eminent way than at other moments and in other persons. . . . It is even without doubt legitimate to regard the relation in which he [Christ] stood to God as absolutely unique, not only as to degree but also as to its essential quality."[1]

Once more, I think religion ought to count exorcised that other philosophical spectre, which affirms a necessary contradiction between the terms Infinite and personality. Of course, if

[1] *Outlines of the Philosophy of Religion,* pp. 149, 150.

one starts, as Paulsen does, with a definition of personality as "the form peculiar to human life," that by hypothesis restricts it to the finite, it is easy to prove that such personality cannot belong to the Infinite.   But the continuation of Paulsen's own argument, though he calls his view "pantheistic," really shows that he himself cannot rest there: "Pantheism, as we understand it, has no intention of depriving God of anything or of denying him anything but human limitations.   It will not permit us to define God by the concept of personality, simply because the notion is too narrow for the infinite fulness and depth of his being.   Still, in order to remove the apprehension, we might call God a *supra-personal* being, not intending thereby to define his essence, but to indicate that God's nature is above the human mind, not below it. And Pantheism might add that it finds no fault with anyone for calling God a personal being in this sense.   Insomuch as the human mind is the highest and most important thing that we know, we can form an idea of God only by intensifying human attributes. . . . . That is *the possible and inevitable anthropomorphism of all religions.*"[1]

It seems wholly legitimate not only but,

[1] Paulsen: *Introduction to Philosophy*, pp. 254, 255.

for our ultimate thinking, far more satisfactory to say, as Lotze essentially does, that
the fact is, that so far from being true that
personality is inconsistent with the Infinite, it
is rather true that personality can be regarded
as complete and perfect only in the Infinite. He
alone, whose being is not bestowed by another
and therefore in much necessarily hidden; he
alone, who is not a mere part in a whole; he
alone, whose memory may infallibly gather all
the past; he alone, whose life is absolutely self-
conditioned—he alone can have complete self-
consciousness and perfect freedom, can thus be
a perfect personality.[1] The terms Infinite and
personal, thus, do not seem to me contradictory.

Moreover, it is to be remembered that the
alternative conceptions, suggested by such terms
as "Impersonal Spirit," "Moral World Order,"
"Infinite Substance," "Self-developing Idea,"
we are really not able to think at all without
at least tacit reference to the notion of personal
spirit. It may well be, that God transcends all
our highest thought, and in this sense may be
called "supra-personal," though this is for us
wholly empty of content; but our highest possible conception of him, nevertheless, is as personal.

[1] Cf. King: *Reconstruction in Theology,* pp. 209-210.

Perhaps no one in modern literature has indicated more effectively the legitimacy of this argument, from the best in the human to the divine, than Browning, in the latter part of his "Saul." This is hardly less than a consummate study of the way by which inspiration may come, and its resulting mood. The whole theme of the latter part of the poem is that God cannot be less than man at his best, even in man's willingness to suffer for love's sake. And the whole world seems to David, in Browning's closing paragraph, to feel the awe of this revelation, and to throb with this vision of an infinitely loving, suffering God:

"I believe it! 'Tis thou, God, that givest, 'tis I who receive:
  In the first is the last, in thy will is my power to believe."

"See the King—I would help him but cannot, the wishes fall
      through.
  Could I wrestle to raise him from sorrow, grow poor to enrich,
  To fill up his life, starve my own out, I would—knowing which,
  I know that my service is perfect.
  Oh, speak through me now!
  Would I suffer for him that I love?
  So wouldst thou—so wilt thou!
  So shall crown thee the topmost, ineffablest, uttermost crown—
  And thy love fill infinitude wholly, nor leave up nor down
  One spot for the creature to stand in!"

Browning often argues that will is more than power, and love than will; and that God cannot be less in any of these ways than man at his best. We have no higher capacities for the true vision of God than exactly the divinest qualities in ourselves,—the qualities of a seeking, suffering, self-giving love. This is a fully justified part of that "inevitable anthropomorphism of all religions" of which Paulsen speaks. No philosophical inheritances need be regarded as invalidating the essence of this contention.

XII

THE DIFFERENCE BETWEEN THE SCIENTIFIC AND RELIGIOUS PROBLEMS

We have now passed in review the misconceptions, injurious to the spiritual life, which arise from ignoring the likeness and connections of the spiritual life with the rest of life. And we turn now to note the misconceptions which come from ignoring the real difference of the spiritual life, its unique sphere and contribution.

In the first place, we may get into great darkness from forgetting that the problems of religious faith have certain distinctive differences from those in natural science; for to forget these differences is to expect an impossible solution in religion.

This means, if we are to keep clear of delusion here, we must, first, carefully observe *science's threefold restriction of itself* to experience, to the tracing of purely causal connections, and to phenomena.

The restriction to experience implies a clear recognition of the fact that science cannot in any case anticipate results independent of previous experience in the same or similar lines. And this really means that the *full cause* of the next stage in the observed process is not present for it in the stage now under observation, in even the most favorable cases. Hume is right, here, in asserting that, in truth, we never really see the causal connection. At most only a part of the conditions disclose themselves to even the finest scientific analysis in the finite things and properties. It seems plain that in this aspect, then, natural science itself looks to and requires an ultimate ideal view to complete it.

The restriction to the tracing of purely causal connections—though even this, as we have just seen, is not ultimate—means that the one great question for natural science is the question of process—how the thing came to be—of mechanical explanation, not the question of meaning. Thus, to use Paulsen's illustration, there are two quite different questions as to a page of print: How did it come to be, what were the processes involved? and what does the page mean? Now the question as to process is the question of science. But the religious question is primarily and necessarily one of *meaning,* of ideal interpretation. This distinction holds, although it is to be not only granted but asserted, that in an ultimate philosophical view the two questions cannot be kept absolutely apart; there we must ask as to their mutual relations. Now it is to be observed that religion's question of the *meaning* of things cannot be solved in the same way as science's question of *process;* though religion, desiring to know exactly how God has acted, must take full account of all the facts brought out by scientific investigation, and must grant absolute freedom of investigation. But when all science's facts of process are fully set forth, the question of their meaning still remains unanswered; and the precise point now to be noted, I repeat, is that this question of meaning that presses upon the religious inquiry, it is impossible to answer in the same way as the scientific question of process. The attempt, therefore, to solve the problem of religious thinking and living *just as* the scientific problem is solved, is foredoomed to failure. We can know beforehand that such a solution is impossible. The two problems differ widely.

Once more, science's restriction of itself to phenomena means that all *ultimate* questions are left out of account as not *so* reachable. It is this very fact, probably, that makes it so easily possible for scientific investigators, when they turn from strict scientific inquiry to philo-

6

sophical questions, to lose sight of the far reaching character of the assumptions involved in terms which they use as matters of course. A method of investigation that deliberately—and for its own limited questions, wisely—ignores all ultimate problems evidently will not solve these ultimate problems. Upon these we can get light only by extended inference from ascertained facts, guided by the laws and demands of our own being. Even a single science, like chemistry, when it tries to become in its own sphere a rational system of thought, is obliged to go quite beyond the phenomenal and bring in much of hypothesis and distant inference.

From the point of view, then, of any one of science's own three restrictions of itself, it is plain that the religious problem is not the same as the scientific problem, and hence cannot be solved in the same way. Science, therefore, *as such,* does not bar the way to faith.

Moreover, in tracing out the difference between the scientific and religious problem, it is worth noting that science itself is an ideal construction of the world—an attempt to think the world into unity in mathematico-mechanical terms. That is, science is itself an ideal which the mind freely creates, cherishes, and seeks to realize; and, as itself such an ideal, cannot, to follow Münsterberg's thought, legitimately rule out other ideals—æsthetic, ethical, or religious. Rather, as James suggests, the comparative success of science is an encouragement in the pursuit of the other more difficult ideals of thinking the world into unity in æsthetic, ethical, or religious terms.

Once more, the scientific problem may be called a *purely intellectual* one; although even here, in the highest scientific questions, imagination must be used; and Lange, though the sympathetic historian of materialism, believed that the greatest scientific discoveries have always been made by those who worked from the point of view of the ideal. Still, in general, it may be truly affirmed that the scientific problem is a purely intellectual one. In such investigations one may wisely set aside all reference to feeling and volition. The question is simply one of exact intellectual formulation, where any obtrusive feeling, or thought of extraneous purpose would only hinder the result.

That is never true of really ultimate questions, and never true in real living. We have already seen that even the problem of pure knowing cannot be solved in merely intellectual terms. While, then, in its proximate inquiries, natural science may very properly cultivate the coldly intellectual mood and ignore all other appeals; for religion to do so would be to take the thoroughly unscientific position of ignoring most important data, and so making a true solution impossible. This is no attempt to evade truth, but the "appeal from a partial and fragmentary truth to a fuller truth." The contrast between scientific and religious faith may, perhaps, be put in this form: scientific faith takes account, and needs to take account, only of intellectual data; while religious faith takes account of the data involved in the feeling of dependence, in æsthetic feelings and in ethical feelings. Where these are overlooked, naturally, as Lotze says, "a very barren rationalism takes the place of that which the whole reason, acting in all directions would be able to produce."[1] "The whole man is the organ of the spiritual."

[1] *Outlines of Philosophy of Religion*, p. 7.

XIII

THE DIFFERENCE BETWEEN THE PHILO-
SOPHICAL AND RELIGIOUS PROBLEMS

But difficulty for the spiritual life and thought may come, also, from ignoring the difference of the religious problem from the philosophical problem, as ordinarily conceived. I am confident, that many serious difficulties arise from the silent assumption, even on the part of theistic and Christian thinkers, that philosophy as commonly conceived is an inference from all accessible data; but this assumption is plainly erroneous. We forget that philosophy, as commonly taught, even in our avowedly Christian colleges, intentionally ignores and abstracts from all those facts that are involved in what we call historical revelation.

Now, it cannot be doubted that it is a perfectly legitimate and valuable question to ask, What may I learn about the ultimate source of things, about the meaning of the world and men, wholly apart from the facts of the so-called historical revelation? But we may never forget that the question so put is a partial one, and deliberately sets aside the most important and vital facts of the world—the preëminent spiritual facts of the race, the world's greatest teachers, as a matter of fact, in religion. It simply puts outside of its data such very significant and indubitable facts—on any possible theory—as Amos, Hosea, Isaiah, and Jesus. Now a philosophy, I submit, that ignores these facts, is plainly not all-embracing in its survey of data, and, therefore, in the nature of the case, cannot expect a complete solution, and cannot be an adequate final philosophy for life or thought.

If, however, we choose to restrict the term philosophy, as is commonly done, to the partial inquiry which ignores the most stupendous facts of the race—and I do not quarrel with the usage, provided we clearly understand it—then philosophy must look to theology for its own completion, as the only systematic inquiry that means in very truth to build upon all the data. I know nothing that, on either scientific or philosophical grounds, can justify us in expecting a satisfactory conclusion from an inquiry into the meaning of the world, that totally ignores the supremely significant fact of the world—the man Jesus, to say nothing of the line of prophets that preceded him. Whatever one's point of view, as data for a discernment of the meaning of things, these great personalities, it would seem, ought to count quite as much as things and events. And Paulsen is not without some perception of this fact; for, after speaking of various dogmas and opinions often asserted to be of the essence of Christianity, he can say, "But if I am allowed to say what I mean and to believe what I can understand and conceive, then, unmindful of the ridicule of the scoffer and the hatred of the guardian of literalism, I may, even in our days, confess to a belief in God who has revealed himself in Jesus. The life and death of Jesus make plain to me the meaning of life, the meaning of all things in general; but that which enables me to live and shows me the import of life I call God and the manifestation of God. The most upright, truthful, and liberal-minded man may subscribe to all that, to-day, as openly as ever before."[1]

Let the thinker and seeker in religion, then, simply take account of the common restriction of philosophy, as it has already taken account of science's self-restriction. These restrictions do not hold for the spiritual life, and do not and cannot bind it in its conclusions. The

---

[1] Paulsen: *Introduction to Philosophy*, pp. 250-251.

spiritual can and must regard all data, and ask the final questions.

It may not be in vain, in concluding the discussion upon the difference of the religious problem and knowledge from the scientific and philosophical, to summarize briefly the relations of science and philosophy to theology, as I conceive them.

Both philosophy and theology raise ultimate questions,—that is, are not confined to phenomena. Both deal with ideal interpretation, rather than mechanical explanation. Philosophy is the science of sciences, as using all sciences (properly including that of religion) as its data; but it raises questions outside the range of science proper.

So theology uses especially data from the science of religion, and in this sense is a science; but it raises questions beyond that or any other science.

A really adequate philosophy would have to take account of all facts, including those of the history of all religions, preëminently the greatest, and must culminate in the question of God. So conceived, philosophy would include theology.

But, as commonly conceived, philosophy excludes all the facts of revelation, and therefore, to complete itself, must look to theology. Theology, then, becomes the crown and culmination of both science and philosophy—itself both a science and philosophy of religion and of God, who is the ultimate explanation of all.

The difference of the religious problem from the æsthetic and ethical can be best seen in the later study of the natural conditions of the spiritual life.

In the consideration of the removable causes of the seeming unreality of the spiritual life, we turn now to the discussion of the unreality which is due to mistaking the nature of the spiritual life itself.

XIV

THE SPIRITUAL LIFE NOT A LIFE OF STRAIN

From these inherited difficulties, which affect both religious thinking and living, we turn to another class of misconceptions particularly affecting concrete religious living, and which arise from mistaking the nature of the spiritual life itself, as a life of strain, or a life of imitation or repetition of others' experiences, or a life of magical inheritance, or, finally, a life of rules laid on from without. These misconceptions follow plainly from ignoring the great fundamental psychical conditions already reviewed; but they influence so powerfully the spiritual life, and end so inevitably in a sense of its unreality, that they deserve to be thus brought together, and definitely set aside.

And, first, the spiritual life is not a life of strain, either in the sense of putting pressure upon the mind to hold certain beliefs, or in the sense of keeping up a certain continuous stress of attention. It *is* a real struggle, a continuing conflict, a life of steady facing of duty; but still it should not be, in any hysterical sense, a life of strain.

This means, in the first place, that the man who wishes to have the spiritual life a reality to him, will not bring any pressure upon his mind to hold certain beliefs. He will rather see clearly that his sole responsibility is simply to put himself face to face with the great realities, and to make an honest response to them. He is honestly to give them their opportunity with him, through earnest attention to the truth; but that is all; he can make no great convictions to order. It should need no argument to cause us to admit, with Dr. Bushnell, that to put pressure on the mind, for whatever end, is, to begin with, dishonest; and we cannot rationally hope that dishonesty will help to the sense of the reality of a spiritual life, that must be from the bottom ethical. Dishonesty, in any form, is itself hollow and false; it is impossible that it should give finally any genuine reality.

Moreover, for this very reason, even when through mere effort of the will a temporary sense of reality is given, a reaction is certain to follow, that leaves the spiritual life less assured than at first. In a word, in every such putting of pressure upon the mind to believe certain things, there is always some latent sense of pretense and unreality, that can never give a solid foundation for spiritual living. The

spiritual life calls for no such straining to believe, and only suffers by it.

The general Protestant procedure of requiring, as the initial step in the religious life, acceptance of a whole system of doctrines, has been
misleading, and has tended distinctly to the
deadening of the spiritual life. Some creed,
doubtless, is implied in all true living; but the
beliefs that can free us and give us strength
and courage are not the product of simple resolution, but those that grow out of our own
deepest experience, those that life constantly
verifies and justifies. For the very health of the
spiritual life itself, therefore, there is to be no
straining to believe in certain doctrines, or to
accept certain miracles, no trying to believe
anything. There is to be rather only that alert
and open-minded spirit, that believes what one
must in view of honest attention to the facts.
It is not yours to make free the truth; rather
"the truth shall make you free."

Nor, in the second place, does the spiritual
life call for the keeping up of a certain stress
of feeling, or of attention. There is need of
clear discrimination at this point. The spiritual
life does look, of course, to a persistent, dominant purpose of righteousness, a real surrender
to the will of God; but this does not and can-

not mean the unchanged continuance of some particular psychological state, the constant keeping of some particular thought or object fixed in the attention, or the steady maintenance of some special state of feeling. The attempt to do everything always with God in mind may be taken as an illustration.

This kind of strained and false substitute for a broad, natural, rational, open-minded spiritual life seems to be widely prevalent just now, not only among very earnest and conscientious people within ordinary Christian lines, but particularly among all sorts of dealers in so-called "mental science." Now, it cannot be denied that a hearty conviction of the possibility of self-control was greatly needed by very many people, who had been practically letting themselves go, and consequently had been making no honest, earnest fight for character, and for some real steadiness of life. Perhaps most men need to know and to fulfil the conditions of self-control to a much greater degree than they do—to come to see that character and peace of mind and even health of body are much more subject to their control than they had thought. And, in this multitudinous discussion of our time, some real psychological conditions have, no doubt, been pointed out, and some legitimate help given to many, in which all may rejoice.

But it is to be feared that along with this legitimate help that is scientifically grounded, there has been a much larger amount of mere faddism, that has prescribed some fixed mental state—sometimes stated in very religious terms, and sometimes not—as the one effectual panacea for all ills. So far as this is true—and it is quite too true—this means that multitudes are put into an abnormal attitude of mental strain, that is reflected even in the cast of their countenances, and particularly in their eyes, which have something in them quite akin to the hunted look of the insane. Whatever achievements may for the time lie back of this attitude of strain, you are not able to escape the conviction that there is here something, in truth, not wholly normal, not quite wholesome, something allied to the hysterical, that inevitably suggests that the true solution has not yet been found.

That this should be the impression is quite natural, for this whole conception of the spiritual life as a life of strain, in the first place, requires a psychological impossibility. Neither in body nor in mind are we fitted to maintain a fixed state of feeling or a fixed attitude of attention. The persistent attempt, therefore, is likely to result in a speedy and pretty complete nervous breakdown—cases by no means uncommon—or to bring about something very like the "insistent ideas" of the insane. And in either case, where a radical conscientiousness has pervaded the attempt, when the mood has once passed, it is likely to end in a still more baffled sense of unreality. It is the least conscientious here, who suffer least.

But, probably, most of those whose theory of the religious life involves a life of strain, the psychological impossibility of their theory will not deter. They cannot allow themselves to be so daunted. But it may weigh with them to consider that such a conception of religion reduces it to a thoroughly man-made affair. No doubt, in most cases, this would seem to them the very antithesis of their intention. But it remains true that, however religious the phraseology in which the view is set forth, any theory of the religious life that calls for this sort of psychological tension really leaves God quite out of account. For if God is real at all, and our relation to him is a reality, the conviction of that reality is not to be simply our product, a thing up to which we must strain. There are, no doubt, conditions upon our part to be fulfilled normally and rationally. But the sense of reality of the spiritual world which we are seeking cannot come simply as forced by us, but only as the result of interaction with the great realities themselves. It is wholly true, as has been already insisted upon, that there can be no mere passivity on our part; we do actively coöperate. But it is also true that the activity is never merely, nor even chiefly, ours, if we are dealing with reality here at all. Let us never forget that, in Herrmann's words, "the certainty of God is not the product of human strivings." That must be primarily God's work, done upon certain plain conditions plainly allowed by our normal life. One cannot wisely attempt, either for himself or for others, to do God's work.

One may appeal here confidently to the life of Jesus. Is there the slightest suggestion in his spirit, that his clear sense of the reality of the spiritual world is in any way hysterical? On the contrary, is not the whole temper of his life that of a confident trust, as of one walking in the very presence of God, to whom it were absurd to suggest that the sense of the reality of God depended upon some strained attitude of attention or painfully maintained mood of feeling, and so might vanish at any moment when the tension became too great?

The whole meaning of his life seems rather to say, "God can be counted upon. The life in relation to him is no mere imaginary one, which you are forced to make; it is a real life in which *he* is constantly at work. I am come to give you the most positive assurance upon that point."

XV

THE SPIRITUAL LIFE NOT A LIFE OF IMITATION

It is equally important for us to remember, if the spiritual life is to be real to us, that it is not a life of the imitation or repetition of the experience of others. That we need others here, as elsewhere, is clear. That we come into most that is of value to us, through introduction by some other, is also plain. Nevertheless, if the spiritual world is to have the fullest reality for us—the reality it ought to have for a mind awakened to mature self-consciousness—we must have some experience in the spiritual that is genuinely our own, not a hollow echo of something we have heard from others.

In a Christian community, where the language of religious experience is familiar, perhaps there is no greater danger besetting the spiritual life than this danger of merely imitating the experience of others. To face the reality of a genuine religious experience, heartily to fulfil the conditions upon which alone it may become genuinely ours, means much that is uncomfortable—real willingness to see the facts of our own life and need as they are, the breaking down of our pride, the giving up of our selfishness and self-indulgence, the putting of ourselves really and persistently in the presence of God's supreme revelation in Christ. This is not easy. Men naturally shrink from it. It is far easier to satisfy oneself with a very shallow dealing with the problem of our life, and then to catch up the traditional language of religious experience from others.

This temptation, in the individual himself, is increased by the virtual demand that has been very generally made by the Church, that there must be a full expression of the meaning of the Christian life at the very beginning, or even as a condition of entering upon it at all. But how is it possible that this should honestly be? It seems very like requiring a student to pass upon a course as a condition of entering it. A confession of Christ that means anything must be one's own, the honest expression of what one has already found Christ to be. A confession of faith requires that the faith—the living experience—should be there, before we confess it. But how can a man confess the divinity of Christ, for example, as a condition of becoming a disciple of Christ? The only confession of Christ's divinity, that can be even approxi-

mately adequate, can come only in his disciple-
ship, in one's deepening experience of what
Christ has come to be to him. Plainly, Christ's
own little circle of the twelve came only gradually, under association with him, to any adequate confession of him. We have no right to
require more. The point of insistence is, not
that we should accept the creed of the apostles
in order to come into their experience, but
rather that we should seek an experience like
the apostles, that may fruit in a like confession,
which can then be genuinely our own.

The very familiarity with the language of
religious experience, then, the instinctive temptation to catch up the expression of life
rather than to insist upon the life itself, and
the demand of the Church for an expression
of Christian life quite beyond the possibility
of experience,—all combine to produce the far
too general habit of expressing more than has
been personally known and experienced, and
hence to give the sense of unreality. This is,
to my mind, the most serious danger, for example, of the Christian Endeavor pledge, particularly with those quite young, where the
matter is not carefully guarded. They are
pledged to speak, whether they have really something of their own to say or not. They naturally

catch up the language of Christian experience, which they have heard from others. Gradually, if they are thoughtful and conscientious and have not been making unusual growth, they come to feel that their language is no true reflection of their own experience. They feel its hollowness; a reaction sets in; and a most depressing sense of the unreality of the spiritual life naturally succeeds. We must not shut our eyes to such dangers. In any case, wherever the religious life becomes, to any large degree, a life of mere imitation or repetition of others' experiences, and the person is at all thoughtful, there the spiritual life is certain to come to seem thoroughly unreal.

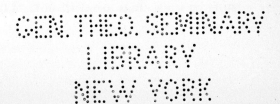

XVI

THE SPIRITUAL LIFE NOT A LIFE OF
MAGICAL INHERITANCE

A third misconception of the nature of the
spiritual life, which is certain finally to give
the sense of its unreality, is that it is a life of
magical inheritance of results.

Our own time is particularly liable to have
this feeling. So far as the scientific spirit really
affects men, they are certain to give increasing
emphasis to the necessity, in all spheres, of the
recognition of laws, of conditions, and of time.
If results in the spiritual life, therefore, are
conceived as coming without clear conditions,
in a kind of merely magical way, that life
unavoidably takes on for such minds a decided
aspect of unreality. It has no intelligible connection with the rest of their life, and there
seems to be nothing they can do with it. This
makes it imperative that those, who would make
the spiritual world a reality for the most wide-
awake minds of our time, must themselves see
the spiritual life as a genuine sphere of laws,
with its own clear conditions that can be known

and stated and fulfilled, with a certainty of results following.   It is not the frills of scientific
illustration that the interpreter of the spiritual
life needs to-day, but the genuine scientific
spirit in the study of his own greatest sphere.
Drummond's greatest contribution to the
thought of his time lay just here.   And there
is still great opportunity for a thoughtful carrying on of his central contention of law in the
spiritual world.

And even for those who are not consciously,
and perhaps not at all, affected by the scientific
temper of our times, there is a similar baffling
sense of the unreality of spiritual things, if the
magical conception largely prevails.   Even such
must have the sense that, in their religious life,
they are simply feeling around in the dark.
What may result, they can have no idea; much
disappointment is certain; they can only hope
that here and there something of what they
seek may be stumbled upon.   And when even
such minds turn to the ordinary avocations of
their lives, and note how confidently they may
count upon results following upon conditions,
they can hardly fail to contrast the sharp outlines of this real life of work with the dimness
of the spiritual.

And none of us may forget without distinct

and large loss that the spiritual life, like all life, is a growth, always involving laws, conditions, and time.   To forget or ignore this, is to make it certain that the spiritual life will become unreal to us.   That is simply to say that we are bound to take account of the common psychological conditions of our life, already considered, and particularly to note the special laws of the spiritual life itself, to be considered later.   These laws, in a word, are the laws of a deepening personal relation, which every day's true living makes better known.

XVII

THE SPIRITUAL LIFE NOT A LIFE OF
EXTERNAL RULES

But if we are not to make the mistake of thinking of the spiritual life as a life of magical inheritance, but rather as clearly involving laws and conditions, neither are we to make the opposite mistake of conceiving the spiritual life as a life of rules laid on from without. Counsels to be heeded there certainly are in the religious life, and valuable habits to be formed. Nevertheless, the heart of the life with God can never be contained in any prescribed routine of rules and regulations. We are called to a real *life,* with its own spontaneous growth and varied expressions, and we are called to *liberty*. Christ seems to have been concerned, not to give rules for holy living or for holy dying, but to trust all to the dynamic of the single motive of love to his person. His disciples are simply asked to be in truth disciples—doing only what loving loyalty to him would suggest. In the liberty of a loyal love, freely won and freely given, they are to live out their lives. No rules have any binding authority which this love does not inspire; and they have even secondary authority, only so long as they are valuable means for that love.

The very essence of the spiritual life is a personal relation with God. No more than any other personal relation can this be wisely made a mere matter of rules. And just as any other personal relation, this relation to God in the religious life will lose its spontaneity, its joy, its growth, and its reality, when external rules are made to determine all. Even in the development of a personal relation, there are clear laws, as we must later notice; but they are the laws of a spontaneously developing life, not external rules laid on from without.

The spiritual life always suffers, and loses in reality, from an extreme emphasis upon the mechanical rules of living, however good the rules in themselves may be. In what is perhaps his most important single address—"The Changed Life"—Drummond states incisively the failure of the method of external rules: "All these methods that have been named—the self-sufficient method, the self-crucifixion method, the mimetic method, and the diary method—are perfectly human, perfectly natural, perfectly ignorant, and, as they stand, perfectly inadequate. Their harm is that they distract attention from the true working method, and secure a fair result at the expense of the perfect one." "The solution of the problem of sanctification is compressed into a sentence—Reflect the character of Christ and you will become like Christ."

Much religious literature, on account of its emphasis on rules of living, has had, thus, particularly in the case of the especially conscientious, a positively deadening effect. So much is made of the machinery, that the man ends with the feeling that it is all machinery, and he is simply going through the motions of life, instead of having the real life itself. This is particularly true, where the rules enjoin much introspection, under which necessarily the very form of the inner life changes. Thoughtful and conscientious religious workers, who have made a great deal of the organization and machinery of their work, are not unlikely to get a similar paralyzing sense that the results are all machine-made. For the sake of the reality of the spiritual life, then, let us not come into bondage to external rules. They are, at the very best, means only, absolutely subordinate in significance.

If now, we definitely set aside in thought and act these four mistaken conceptions of the nature of the spiritual life, as a life of strain, of imitation, of magical inheritance, and of rules from without, we shall have done something to insure its greater reality: and as over against these false conceptions, we shall set the thought of a life, normal, real, effective, free.

These mistaken conceptions of the nature of the spiritual life themselves suggest that perhaps the greatest source of the seeming unreality of the spiritual life is the simple failure to fulfil its natural conditions.

FAILURE TO FULFIL CONDITIONS

XVIII

THE WAY INTO THE GREAT VALUES

Plainly, if the spiritual life is a true sphere of normal living at all, it must have its natural conditions, and failure to fulfil these conditions must result in the spiritual life becoming unreal. The very fact that the religious life is so intimately concerned with æsthetic and ethical data makes it certain that the natural conditions of the spiritual life will have a marked similiarity to the conditions of recognizing and entering into any sphere of value. And the fact that the religious life is essentially a personal relation with God, and that Christ's great commandment is love for God and for men, makes it equally certain that the conditions of the spiritual life are essentially the same as the conditions of a deepening personal relation.

Here, too, we may well note how far the conditions of the spiritual life are similar to the conditions of æsthetic appreciation, and to the conditions of a deepening personal relation, and how far the conditions of the spiritual life are different.

If one asks first, then, how it is that we

generally come into the great spheres of value,—
of music, and literature, and art, and friendship, he must recognize that, in all alike, we are
commonly introduced through the witness of
some other, who has already found his way into
an appreciation of the value. One who should
insist on discovering all values at first hand
would inevitably doom himself to a very narrow life. We naturally count, therefore, in all
these spheres of value, on our inheritance from
the past, and upon the certainty that others may
have already found what we would gladly find.
If, then, in our spiritual life we are ignoring
entirely the witness of others, if we are not at
all putting ourselves where we would naturally
get that witness, we need not wonder that we
are not making the progress that would otherwise be possible.

In like manner, to come into any one of these
great values requires on our own part absolute
honesty, coupled with a genuine modesty. On
the one hand, there is to be no pretense of
having reached a degree of appreciation that is
not yet ours. This can only hinder our growth
into any value. We shall not, therefore, simply
catch up the opinions of others as our own, but
speak honestly only of that which we have ourselves attained. But on the other hand, with

an equally real modesty, we shall not claim
that we ourselves have seen all that there is in
any of these spheres of value. Doubtless there
is much more than we have yet appreciated,
and we shall not, therefore, make what we have
already seen the measure of all reality. We
may modestly hope that much that others have
found, that we cannot honestly claim yet to
have discovered for ourselves, may still come
to us if we continue to give the great values
honest opportunity with us. Here, too, that is,
our spiritual life may have suffered through our
lack of this absolute honesty, on the one hand,
or of this genuine modesty on the other.

These very qualities themselves suggest that
one great method of coming into a sense of
reality and achievement in any of the great
spheres of value is, that we should simply stay
persistently in the presence of the best in the
sphere in which we seek attainment, in honest
response to that best. There need be no pretense.
We are called simply to give attention, time,
and thought; the great realities and values will,
thus, finally verify themselves. But where one
has given a great value no opportunity to make
its own legitimate impression, he cannot wonder
that the sense of its reality and significance is
lacking. We have no right to expect conviction

8

and sense of value where we have not given the best an honest chance at us. Probably the greatest reason for failure in the sense of reality and achievement in the spiritual life, as in the case of all other values, lies just here. And it is thus, above all, that "the inner light fails."

In trying, now, to transfer to the religious life the conditions of entering upon any sphere of value, how far must *differences* be recognized?

We have seen that even in the case of æsthetic appreciation, conditions essentially ethical, like honesty and modesty, could not be ignored. And yet, doubtless, in æsthetic appreciation, the ethical is not so intrinsically involved as in the religious life; and this is the particular point at which the analogy needs careful guarding.

The religious life can never be one of mere passive appreciation, or æsthetic admiration; it requires through and through the active ethical will. The revelation of God in Christ is preëminently the revelation of an ethical will —of character; and such a revelation makes demands upon one; it is a constant appeal to conscience, a persistent motive to willing. It inevitably asks, What are you going to do with that will and life? "Will we willingly surrender to the spiritual power whose influence

we thus perceive to be all around us? Or will
we treat this incomparable thing as an every-
day matter and in laziness forget it and turn
our backs on it? This, at last, is the real test-
question of faith. And it passes over immediately into the other question, whether or not
we are willing to be sincere."[1] The very existence of harmonious personal relation to God
requires such an ethical will in the worshipper.
The character of God, then, can never be a
mere subject of passive æsthetic admiration; it
demands a moral surrender to the will of God,
and strenuous endeavor to embody that will in
life.

That persistent staying in the presence of
the worthful, therefore, which æsthetic appreciation requires as its chief condition, in the
case of the religious life must mean more than
a passive waiting. The religious life must
recognize, indeed, as we have seen, that the resulting conviction is not simply its own product;
but still there must be active, hearty, loyal co-
operation with the divine will, a prompt following of all light revealed. Nothing less than
this is really giving God and the spiritual world
a chance at us. The religious life is so inevi-

[1] Herrmann: *Communion with God,* p. 83.

tably and indubitably knit up with the ethical,[1] that there can be no doubt as to this difference of the conditions of the spiritual life from those of æsthetic appreciation.

But, with this point guarded, the analogy of the growing appreciation of any sphere of value has continual suggestion for the spiritual life, that may save it from much perplexity and from serious blunders, and may bring it rather to some clear insight into its own laws.

[1] See King: *Theology and the Social Consciousness,* Chap. VII.

XIX

THE CONDITIONS OF A DEEPENING
PERSONAL RELATION

It is perhaps still more obvious that, if the relation to God is a personal relation at all, the laws of the spiritual life must be primarily the laws of a deepening personal relation; and that, wherever any soul is ignoring such a deepening relation with God and with men, he is making it inevitable that the spiritual life should seem to him unreal, and that he should have no sense of growth and achievement in it.

To state, then, simply, the conditions upon which a personal relation with God and with men would deepen, would be to state the fundamental laws of the spiritual life. If one is ignoring these laws, he need not wonder that the spiritual world is for him obscure.

It is not difficult to summarize, at least suggestively, what these conditions of any deepening personal relation must be; for it is plain that every friendship worthy the name must build upon mutual self-revelation and answering trust, mutual self-giving, and some deep community of interests. If we are not laying this foundation in our relations to God and to men, we are naturally making it impossible that there should be reality and depth in the relations involved in our religious life. One needs, this means, to put himself honestly face to face with God's great self-revelation in Christ, to give himself in real ethical activity in this relation, and to seek the great interests of the kingdom of God that lie at God's own heart. Only so is a real basis laid for steady growth into the divine friendship.

And when one asks how in any personal relation he may go forward to build upon this foundation, exactly the same suggestions, that may be made concerning any human relation, will be found to bear directly upon growth into the life with God. We must, for example, count upon unconscious growth here rather than conscious arrangement. We may not expect continuous emotion, but must rely mainly upon steady association with the life of Christ. We shall see that this personal relation, like any other, will grow naturally by the expression of it in the various ways possible to us, and we shall be sure to be genuine throughout.

That is, in a word, this whole analogy of the religious life to a personal relation suggests definite and deep, but yet simple, conditions

that we may know and fulfil, and, in the fulfilment of them, be able to count upon results.
But this must mean, also, that, where these plain
conditions of a deepening personal relation are
ignored, the spiritual life cannot be real or
significant.

When we pass to the consideration of the
differences between the conditions of the religious life and those of any other deepening personal relation, we are led here, too, to see that,
just because this conception of the religious life
as a personal relation has such deep significance,
it is the more necessary that we should not
unwarrantably transfer to the relation to God
those limitations which, because of our very
finiteness, hold in the relation of finite to finite.
We are, then, carefully to guard the conception,
making it clear to ourselves that we are seeking
a relation to a God who has concretely and objec-
tively revealed himself in Christ; and that we
are not, therefore, to enter upon the experiment
of simply building up a subjective experience
of our own.

Not less are we to remember that we cannot,
of course, expect a sensuous relation to God
like that which accompanies, rather than constitutes, our true spiritual relation to other persons.   Nor should this analogy mean that there

is to be any failure in the deepest reverence; in claiming this personal relation to God we do not, and we may not, put ourselves upon familiar equality with God. And we shall especially remember that the relation to God, just because of what God is, must have a universality all its own. Since God is the God of perfect righteousness and life, and is himself the source of the moral constitution of men, the relation to him cannot be conceived sentimentally, but naturally carries with it our relations to all other personalities. The relation to God is that one relation which, itself set right, sets all other relations right. And there can be, therefore, no such thing as a growing religious life that does not mean at the same time a life of increasing faithfulness in all our human relations.

THE INEVITABLE LIMITATIONS AND FLUC-
TUATIONS OF OUR NATURES

XX

LIMITATIONS AND FLUCTUATIONS
COMMON TO ALL OUR LIFE

From the removable causes of the seeming
unreality of the spiritual life we turn, now, to
the study of the second class of causes of this
sense of unreality, which, while not removable,
are still recognizable. These unremovable causes
may, perhaps, be reduced to two: the inevitable
limitations and fluctuations of our natures, and
our need of training in the moral and religious
life. In the consideration of both, we may again
profitably observe how far the spiritual life is
here similar to other spheres of life, and how
far, different.

It need hardly be said how large is the
warrant for finding in our inevitable limitations
some of the most effective causes of the seeming
unreality of the spiritual world. How strong,
for example, in all generations has been the appeal to the thoughtful of Plato's detailed figure
of the cave! And it is interesting to remember
that the most influential of all English philosophical writings, Locke's great *Essay Concerning Human Understanding,* had its rise from

a like conviction of the necessary influence of our natural limitations. Locke's own account of the matter in his "epistle to the reader" is worth recalling: "Were it fit to trouble thee with the history of this *Essay,* I should tell thee that five or six friends meeting at my chamber, and discoursing on a subject very remote from this, found themselves quickly at a stand, by the difficulties that arose on every side. After we had awhile puzzled ourselves, without coming any nearer a resolution of those doubts which perplexed us, it came into my thoughts that we took a wrong course; and that before we set ourselves upon inquiries of that nature, it was necessary to examine our own abilities, and see what objects our understandings were or were not fitted to deal with. This I proposed to the company, who all readily assented; and thereupon it was agreed that this should be our first inquiry. Some hasty, undigested thoughts, on a subject I had never before considered, which I set down against our next meeting, gave the first entrance into this discourse." It is particularly instructive to find, according to the later testimony of one of this memorable company of "five or six friends," that the questions under discussion, which drove Locke to this thought of the inevitable limitations of our understanding, were the "principles of morality and revealed religion."[1]

Any thoughtful consideration of spiritual themes, indeed, must soon bring one to share with Plato and Locke the further conviction that, in striving to reach any rational faith in a world above the senses, we must take full account of those difficulties that are to be expected from the very finiteness of our faculties. These limitations we cannot escape, but clearly to recognize them is itself at least a partial deliverance from their domination.

Let us ask, first, how far these inevitable limitations and fluctuations of our natures produce effects in the spiritual life *similar* to those in other spheres of living.

Our finiteness in itself must in much limit our insight into the spiritual world.

In the first place, in our very nature, we are discursive beings—in thinking and in living, and in all spheres. Nowhere do we have immediate intuitive insight into wholes. The full meaning of every experience is brought to us only bit by bit. And even where in rare moments we seem to get all in an instant, we commonly are later able to see that this moment of vision either had been long preparing, or

[1] Fraser's *Locke,* pp. xvi-xvii.

failed to give us its complete significance until in discursive thinking we had wrought it into the rest of our life.

This finiteness means, too, that our view of the world is necessarily but partial. We do not stand with God at the center of things, to be able to discern the full complex purpose with which each thing is called into being. At best, it must be a very small part of the whole detailed plan, which even with the most careful study we can come to see. Doubtless, in much, as Plato suggested, we are dealing with shadows as though they were the realities. Everywhere this limitation of view confronts us. Not in the most favorable cases are we able to carry our view completely through with certainty. Our ultimate conclusions can have, at best, only practical certainty, a reasonable probability.

It is a distinct help to bear these necessary limitations in mind; for it makes clear the kind and degree of evidence, which alone we have a right to expect anywhere.

In close connection with these inevitable results of our finiteness as such, there is also to be considered the unavoidable influence of bodily and psychical conditions. We are concerned with these here, only so far as they are beyond our control. So far as they are alterable, they have been already dealt with. The conditions being present, we cannot directly change their natural effects. This is a part of our limitation. But, if we can clearly recognize the source of the effects, our final inferences from these effects may be essentially altered.

In no part of our life can we safely ignore the unavoidable effects of bodily conditions. With all possible care of bodily conditions we cannot preserve an unvarying state of body; and changing bodily conditions tinge inevitably our mental states. The careful study of the effects of fatigue, even in sense-perception, gives many an illustration. So, too, the psychical conditions are constantly changing. And with this constant change, however produced, we have always to reckon. That nothing in life should seem always the same to us, is the inevitable result. We are to expect, therefore, from both physical and psychical conditions, changing vital feelings, alternation of moods, altering power of attention, and some consequent ebb and flow in conviction and in the sense of reality. We need not regard this as wholly a weakness; it is in part, at least, an evidence of the breadth of our natures. We are made on so broad and unified a plan, that we cannot come to our best in anything, without taking all sides of our nature into account. But, in any case, we have this fluctuation in the sense of reality to face.

Inevitably, thus, our vital feelings will change, and with them our general sense of the reality of things; for feeling is perhaps the strongest element in the living sense of reality.

Even independently of the more strictly physical vital feelings, in our very nature as psychical beings, we are creatures of moods with their inevitable flux, and this cannot be without its influence upon our sense of reality. So long as feeling enters necessarily so much into our sense of the reality of all things, the things of the spirit especially, which do not force themselves upon us, will vary for us in their clearness and reality. This cannot be wholly avoided. The spiritual life simply shares here with all life the influence of the changing moods.

Moreover, so far as change in nervous energy affects power of attention, it will affect our proportionate emphasis upon things, and so again our sense of their reality.

But, in all this, let it be repeated, we have nothing that is peculiar to the religious life. It holds for all spheres of value, and, indeed, in every sphere of life where feeling enters at all. This really implies that, wherever we are not living a merely fragmentary life, this ebb and flow of feeling and hence of the sense of reality must be reckoned with; it is involved in our very natures as finite and feeling beings. Let us not suppose, then, that we confront here a difficulty in any way peculiar to the religious life. Are there no hours when the life of mere worldly culture, too, seems flat, stale, and unprofitable, when a sense of unreality comes as to the best in literature, in music, and in art, and one does not feel adequate to them? Is it not rather true that there is needed a constant struggle to maintain the highest standards in these spheres as truly as in the religious, whether in an individual, in a community, or in an institution of learning?

Moreover, the life of the rejection of all ideals, and the life of unbelief, have their fluctuations, too. It is not merely the conviction of the highest which varies. The lower life, also, has its inevitable misgivings. We are creatures of two worlds, an animal and a spiritual; and both make themselves felt in some degree. Unbelief has its questionings as well as belief. The situation is not, as seems so often tacitly assumed, that, if we once gave

9

up our ideals, we should then rest satisfied, quite without qualm, or misgiving, or questioning. The truth is rather that, being citizens of two worlds, we cannot wholly escape the influence of either. We may not choose whether our life shall vary or not. We can only choose the dominant moods. If we turn from the life of faith, we have at most, as Browning makes Bishop Blougram point out, substituted

> "A life of doubt diversified by faith
> For one of faith diversified by doubt.
> We called the chess-board white; we call it black."

XXI

THE SPECIAL BEARING OF LIMITATIONS AND FLUCTUATIONS ON THE SPIRITUAL LIFE

Thus far, in our consideration of the inevitable limitations of our natures, we have been considering effects which are not peculiar to the spiritual life, but which are essentially the same for all spheres of life. We turn now to ask in what way the religious life is peculiarly affected by these limitations, how far the effects in the spiritual life *differ* from those in other spheres.

The difference, let it be said at once, certainly does not consist, as has been strangely enough sometimes suggested, in the fact that the religious life does not have its sense-manifestations in the world. Plutarch's famous passage concerning the omnipresence of temples and altars would seem to indicate that these manifestations have been plain enough. The reality of the religious life certainly cannot be called in question, on the ground that it has not in the most varied and multiplied ways bodied itself forth to the senses.

Nevertheless, our inevitable limitations and fluctuations undoubtedly do make themselves

felt with peculiar power in our religious thinking and living. That this is natural appears at
once, when one considers the greatness of the
achievement sought to be made in the religious
life; for the greater the task, the less easy must
be its accomplishment.

For, in the first place, we have here most
clearly the finite dealing with the infinite problem. If even in all our finite inquiries we are
burdened with the sense of our limitations,
much more here, where we are avowedly face
to face with the question of the Infinite Life,
must we feel the feebleness of our powers. And
if, even in the inquiry concerning the finite, our
conclusions must fall short of demonstrative
completeness, plainly must we be content in the
inquiry after the Infinite with a reasonable faith.

And yet, even in our inquiries into the finite,
it should be noted, all our questions ultimately
seem to require a final Unity, that is more than
finite; and the deepest convictions of philosophy and religion seem thus necessary to make
finally consistent our proximate conclusions. In
this respect our lesser problems appear really
to depend for their complete solution upon the
greater.

Again, our limitations may naturally affect
us more strongly in the religious life, because

the grounds of our great spiritual convictions must lie deeper than those of less significant opinions. The very fact that the reasons for spiritual life and conviction do not lie on the surface, but are deeply intertwined with the very roots of our being and with the different sides of our nature, particularly the ethical—and if they have any real justification, this must be true—makes these reasons for spiritual life and faith all the less capable of quick and easy statement and appreciation; and so our limitations will be especially felt just here.

Moreover, just because the religious life is so closely knit up with the ethical, the sense of its reality is peculiarly subject to fluctuation. In truth, the sense of the reality of the spiritual life depends, to a degree true of no other sphere of life, upon the ethical attitude. Religious convictions, therefore, are unusually sensitive to one's moral changes. This is, of course, true in part in other spheres of life, on account of the very unity of our being, but by no means to the same extent. Here, then, is a special reason why fluctuation occurs in religious convictions. We cannot cut this bond of connection between religious conviction and moral attitude, but we can change our moral attitude; and just so far this cause of fluctuation belongs with the removable causes. The more stably right our ethical spirit is, the more permanent is our religious faith. I assume here, of course, the justification of the ethical.

For all these reasons, the spiritual life must be preëminently a life of gradual growth and patient, steady endeavor. The greatest things need time, patience, study, a wise use of moods, and persistent earnestness. The maintenance of any of our ideals demands some fighting; but the true man cannot be willing, either for himself or for others, to draw away from these fighting forces—fighting to maintain the highest ideals and faith in them. George MacDonald's rector in the "Quiet Neighborhood" says to his doubting, listless friend, "You know the 'Faery Queen.' Think how long the Red-Cross Knight traveled with the Lady Truth—Una, you know —without learning to believe in her; and how much longer still without ever seeing her face. For my part may God give me strength to follow till I die. Only I will venture to say this, that it is not by any agony of the intellect, that I expect to discover her."

Browning's "Childe Roland" has a different meaning, I suppose, for every mind that reads it; but for me it seems always to contain a marvellous allegory of the dauntless spirit that may well characterize the soul in its quest for spiritual truth and life. An end set and pursued; an end pursued after enthusiasm, confidence, hope had died; pursued after companions had been defeated and had perished; pursued still alone when

> "just to fail as they, seemed best,
> And all the doubt was now—should I be fit?"

yet pursued in darkness, foreboding, doubt; pursued across that dismal ill-omened waste whose first glimpse brings the shudder of utter loneliness, and where the unending ugliness of nature conspires with the temptations within to drive him back; pursued in spite of the deadly horrors of the way, in spite of those last terrors that would cheat of the prize within his grasp, in spite even of the devil-suggested doubt—Why should he hope to conquer, where so many worthy had failed; in spite of all, to the very last, pursued!

> "Dauntless the slug-horn to my lips I set
> And blew 'Childe Roland to the Dark Tower came.'"

XXII

THE WITNESS OF OUR CONSCIOUSLY BEST HOURS

This close connection of the religious and the ethical leads us to emphasize the important principle that, when we find fluctuations in our convictions concerning the reality of anything, we must ask for the witness of our consciously best hours, physically, intellectually, and morally. If religious conviction does tend to go up and down with our moral attitude, and the ethical has any real justification, then our religious convictions are just so far confirmed. And, with reference to the entire man, it behooves us to ask, When does the spiritual world seem most real to us? in our best or our worst moments? when we are consciously most in possession of ourselves in every way, or when we are consciously below our best? So Tyndall, for example, tested the doctrine of material atheism: "I have noticed," he said, "during years of self-observation, that it is not in hours of clearness and vigor that this doctrine commends itself to my mind."[1]

[1] Quoted by Orr, *The Christian View of God and the World*, p. 74.

So far, now, as we can control the conditions—bodily, intellectual, and moral—of our best hours, the ideal world may be truly said to exist for us in the proportion in which we make it to exist. And to just that extent, the fluctuation in our sense of the reality of the spiritual life may be ascribed to removable causes, already considered. But so far as our sense of the reality of the spiritual life is affected by limitations inevitably involved in our finiteness, or by fluctuations in our mental states due to constitutional conditions and connections but very partially subject to our control, the causes are not removable, but they are recognizable. And to see that the wavering sense of spiritual reality is due, not to any lack of realness in the spiritual world, but only to changing conditions in ourselves, is to be delivered from many doubts and fears, and to take a long step toward a confident religious faith. When Kant found that a constant feeling of depression which attended him had its cause in the abnormal narrowness of his chest, he could not throw off the physical feeling, but he could keep it from shadowing his life. So, we need constantly to take account of our necessary finite limitations and the inevitable fluctuations of our life, if we are to keep our religious faith clear and strong.

The very fact, that these unremovable causes of the sense of the unreality of the spiritual life are to be found in our natural constitution, suggests that it may not be intended that the spiritual life should always seem to us equally real and commanding. And if we press the inquiry, Why should this be intended? it seems possible to suggest but one answer consonant with a genuine religious faith: it must be needed as a part of our moral and spiritual training. We are brought, thus, to consider the last of the causes of the seeming unreality of the spiritual life.

A PURPOSED SEEMING UNREALITY OF
THE SPIRITUAL

XXIII

THE SEEMING UNREALITY A LARGE FACTOR IN OUR MORAL AND SPIRITUAL TRAINING

This would mean the recognition that, besides all the causes with which we have been dealing—manifold misconceptions, failure to fulfil the natural conditions, and inevitable limitations and fluctuations—there is another,— a certain purpose, involved in the very constitution of ourselves and of the world, that the reality of the spiritual life shall not be a mere brute fact to be passively grasped once for all, but a living deed, requiring ever to be purposely renewed. For the sake, then, of our moral and spiritual training, for the sake of deepening the spiritual life itself into which the moral is so inextricably woven, there is a purposed seeming unreality in spiritual things.

Even here, where we could least expect it, it is to be noted that there is still a real *similarity* between the spiritual life and the other spheres of life. For it is the distinctive mark of man, as Browning is so fond of insisting, that he is a growing creature. And this appears on every side of his life.

Nowhere is anything done fully to man's hand. He is no "finished and finite clod." He has no "finished instincts." Everywhere he must work out his task. His science, even, is the work of ages, toilsomely wrought out by countless contributors, and is a task always only in the making. As an intellectual product it cannot be inherited, and it is *consciously* shared in, as Lotze notes, by very few; for no man can passively receive it. It is a kingdom to be conquered. So throughout our lives, the best must ever be wrought out.

All the conditions of our life, too, seem adjusted to this thought of an imperfect, growing creature. The almost unbelievable extent to which life everywhere calls for the repetition of acts is evidence. The proverbs of all nations bear witness. The enormous place and power of habit point to the same conclusion. The way in which the most fundamental qualities of character require for their development steady submission to the daily drudgery, is particularly significant. There is evidently no intention, in the constitution of the world or of men, to bring men to any high attainment, except by strenuous endeavor on their own part. We need not think it strange, then, that in the highest life of all, even its reality should be made to depend in no small degree on our constant struggle.

But the fact that points most unmistakably to the seeming unreality of the spiritual world as an intended part of our moral and spiritual training, is that very closely connected deficiency in moral insight which is not without its moral advantage. In Lotze's words: "It would not be advantageous for moral development if the binding truth of all particular moral commands, and the indissoluble connection between them, were presented to individual minds with the theoretical certainty of an arithmetical proof, and if it were not left for every soul to fight its way through the battle of life, by living, believing action and effort, to this clearness of comprehensive moral intuition."[1]

The constant power and attraction of a repeated temptation, the hollowness of which we think we have already fully discovered, seem, thus, to indicate a certain intended deficiency in moral insight. We are not to be spared the needed struggle. We are to keep striving. We come into character only so. Our ethical purpose must be constantly reaffirmed in active resistance to temptations ever renewed. A moral insight, that should rob the temptations of all

[1] *Microcosmus,* Vol. II, p. 54.

power, would take from us the very struggle needed for our moral growth. In this preliminary stage of our training in the earthly life, at least, our best growth comes only so. And life becomes thus everywhere "a godlike challenge in the night to our too reluctant wills."

If this is true in the purely ethical life, we need not wonder that in the religious life also, with which the ethical is so completely bound up, there are intended conditions which continually compel a reaffirming of the spiritual, if it is to be held at all. Even the removable causes of spiritual unreality—manifold misconceptions and failure to fulfil natural conditions —and the necessary recognition of the unremovable limitations and fluctuations,—even these, as we have seen, demand a persistent, thoughtful pursuit of the spiritual. But if to these is to be added a purposed seeming unreality, there is here brought to us a definite challenge to conquer a spiritual kingdom for ourselves.

This point is of such central importance that there may well be added upon it these words of Professor Seth Pattison:[1] "If we are really in earnest, at once with the unity of the world and with the necessity of an intrinsically worthy end by reference to which existence may be

[1] *Man's Place in the Cosmos*, pp. 32-33.

explained, we must take our courage in both hands and carry our convictions to their legitimate conclusion. We must conclude that the end which we recognize as alone worthy of attainment is also the end of existence as such—the open secret of the universe. No man writes more pessimistically than Kant of man's relation to the course of nature, so long as man is regarded merely as a sentient creature, susceptible to pleasure and pain. But man, as the subject of duty, and the heir of immortal hopes, is restored by Kant to that central position in the universe from which, as a merely physical being, Copernicus had degraded him.

"To a certain extent this conclusion must remain a conviction rather than a demonstration, for we cannot emerge altogether from the obscurities of our middle state, and there is much that may rightly disquiet and perplex our minds. But if it is in the needs of the moral life that we find our deepest principle of explanation, then it may be argued with some reason that this belongs to the nature of the case; for a scientific demonstration would not serve the purposes of that life. The truly good man must choose goodness on its own account; he must be ready to serve God for naught, without being invaded by M. Renan's doubts. As it has been finely put, he must possess 'that rude old Norse nobility of soul, which saw virtue and vice alike go unrewarded, and was yet not shaken in its faith.' . . . . But because such is the temper of true virtue, it by no means follows that such virtue will not be rewarded with 'the wages of going on, and not to die.' "

In all this, the conditions of the religious life show a real similarity to those of the rest of life. But there is a certain *difference* in this purposed unreality, now to be observed.

XXIV

THE SPECIAL RELIGIOUS NEED OF THE UN-OBTRUSIVENESS OF THE SPIRITUAL

The chief difference, no doubt, consists in the fact that, in the religious life, we are dealing with the most fundamental of all relations— the relation to God, which, we have already seen, has a universality all its own. Even the ethical life, therefore, so far as it is conceived as independent of the religious, has no such sweep as the religious life. And if the ethical demanded the training of a constantly compelled struggle, this, much more. To come into any worthy personal relation to a God, right relation to whom involves right relation to all others and to all else, is no holiday task. It calls for a girding up of the loins of our minds. "Self-renunciation," à Kempis reminds us, "is not the work of one day, nor children's sport."

Moreover, the simple fact that in the religious life we have to deal with an unseen God, so unobtrusive as to seem almost deliberately to hide his working, gives to the conditions of the religious life some real difference. Here we have not only to maintain ourselves in a spiritual world, plainly given as a fact, but we have almost to maintain the reality of that world itself. We must create, in some real sense, not only our moral spirit, but also the very realm in which that spirit is to be shown. The very existence for us of the spiritual world, that is, seems in no small measure committed to our trust. Day by day we are to assure ourselves anew: There is a God; he does love; man is free; man is immortal; this life is not all; there is a growing, all-embracing Kingdom of God. That religion has in all this a task somewhat, though not wholly, peculiar, will hardly be denied.

But the difference just noted, like the first difference, evidently makes a supreme demand upon the ethical purpose. And the contrast between the conditions of the religious life and those of all the rest of life, except the ethical, as to the intended obscurity with which we have to deal, lies exactly in this inseparableness of the religious and the ethical. The ethical spirit is absolutely essential to the true religious life. There must, therefore, be emphasized in every possible way in the religious life that which will morally train; and the merely formal, perfunctory, or imitated must be sternly eliminated. If there is a God at all, who really intends to bring us to the highest life, we may confidently expect that the conditions of our life will be so shaped as to call out in us the persistent ethical will. In Herrmann's words,[1] "We are to seek communion with God, not as something along-side of devotion to what is good, but only *in* this devotion."

Above all else, this means that the conditions must be such that the religious life may be the man's own, voluntarily chosen and voluntarily kept. If this is to be true, a sacred reverence for the human personality must be a controlling principle in all God's dealing with us. Man's freedom will be respected, and his individuality respected. There will be no over-riding of either in any way. This implies that, in the nature of the case, it is impossible that there should be any forcing of God and the spiritual life upon a man. They must become his own, by voluntary recognition, by persistent choosing. Only so can he keep his spiritual life and grow in it.

And if there is to be no forcing of God and the spiritual world upon a man, this would seem to mean further, that we can expect no absolutely incontrovertible evidences, no over-powering signs—certainly not before the ethical

[1] *Communion with God,* p. 206.

choice. A choice will be left, some room for our own attitude of will to have its effect. It is this principle that Pascal seems to have in mind when he says:[1] "God wished to render himself perfectly recognizable to those who seek him with their whole heart; and hidden from those who shun him with all their heart." "Religion is a thing so great, that it is just that those who would not take the pains to seek it, if it is obscure, should be deprived of it. What do they complain of then, if it is such that they could find it by seeking it?" And he intimates how this obscurity becomes a moral test: "If you care but little to know the truth, here [in a suggested difficulty] is enough to leave you in repose. But if you desire with all your heart to know the truth, it is not enough, examine minutely."

Wherever, then, we ask in the spiritual life for incontrovertible evidence, we ask not only for that which transcends our limitations, but for that which on moral grounds also is not to be granted; we ask that the conditions of our life should be less perfectly adapted than they now are to our highest moral and spiritual needs. The seeming unreality of the spiritual world becomes itself, thus, a ground of trust.

[1] *Thoughts and Letters*, pp, 327, 355.

But even more than this is to be said. Our moral need seems plainly to require, also, that there shall be *no domination of the human personality by God's personality*. Not only will God not thrust the fact of his existence upon us in resistless fashion, whatever our moral attitude, but in his personal relation to us, even after we have voluntarily and gladly recognized it, he will still sacredly respect our own moral initiative and our own individuality. Because he would bring us to real character and to a spiritual experience of our own, he will jealously guard his action, hiding his hand in his dealing with us, not putting upon us the practically irresistible pressure of over-powering personality. If even the parent and elder friend need to take pains not to dominate with their personalities the growing personality of the 'child, much more must the Infinite Personality guard the manifestations of himself. The very possibility of unmistakably genuine character in finite beings seems to depend upon the fact that God should, thus, at least in the preliminary stages of their training, scrupulously remain the indemonstrable, the invisible, the hidden, the unobtrusive God, showing such a reverence for the personality of his children as men never show for one another.

Kant clearly recognizes this imperative need of the hidden God, and his own careful statement deserves quotation:[1] Else "*God* and *eternity* with their *awful majesty* would stand unceasingly *before our eyes,* (for what we can prove perfectly is to us as certain as that of which we are assured by the sight of our eyes). Transgression of the law would no doubt be avoided, what is commanded would be done; but the mental *disposition,* from which actions ought to proceed, cannot be infused by any command, and in this case the spur of action is ever active and *external,* so that reason has no need to exert itself in order to gather strength to resist the inclinations by a lively representation of the dignity of the law: hence most of the actions that conformed to the law would be done from fear, a few only from hope, and none at all from duty, and the moral worth of actions, on which alone in the eyes of supreme wisdom the worth of the person and even that of the world depends, would cease to exist. As long as the nature of man remains what it is, his conduct would thus be changed into mere mechanism, in which, as in a puppet show, everything would *gesticulate* well, but there would be

---

[1] *Dialectic of Pure Practical Reason.* Abbott: *Kant's Theory of Ethics,* pp. 357-358.

no life in the figures. Now, when it is quite otherwise with us, when with all the effort of our reason we have only a very obscure and doubtful view into the future, when the Governor of the world allows us only to conjecture his existence and his majesty, not to behold them or prove them clearly; and on the other hand, the moral law within us, without promising or threatening anything with certainty, demands of us disinterested respect; and only when this respect has become active and dominant, does it allow us by means of it a prospect into the world of the super-sensible, and then only with weak glances: all this being so, there is room for true moral disposition, immediately devoted to the law, and a rational creature can become worthy of sharing in the *summum bonum* that corresponds to the worth of his person and not merely to his actions. Thus what the study of nature and of man teaches us sufficiently elsewhere may well be true here also; that the unsearchable wisdom by which we exist is not less worthy of admiration in what it has denied than in what it has granted."

It is not strange, then, after all, that the spiritual life meets us constantly with the paradoxical demand that we should in some real sense create the objects of our faith, as well as

act in view of them. So Kant felt as to God
and freedom and immortality. So Fichte affirmed as to the entire world of the spirit. So
James has asserted most strongly as to freedom.
So Browning and many another has believed
as to the love of God and all that that involves.
Religion is a deed. And, in a very real sense,
we are left to determine whether for us there
shall be a God, and a loving God, a freedom,
an immortality, a future world, a Kingdom of
God. God has intended that the conditions of
our life should be such as to challenge us at
every point to a stalwart faith and a stalwart
life. As Browning says, thinking of the central
truth of all—the love of God, and his supreme
historical revelation in Christ:

> "So duly, daily, needs provision be
> For keeping the soul's prowess possible,
> Building new barriers as the old decay,
> Saving us from evasion of life's proof,
> Putting the question ever, 'Does God love,
> And will ye hold that truth against the world?'"

And it is impossible to let this truth, of which
we are now speaking, get full possession of us,
and not find a great new light thrown on
the whole dark problem of evil—our greatest
natural obstacle to a satisfying religious faith.
Seeing how much is at stake in this reverent
guarding, at any cost, of our moral initiative

and of our individuality, we learn not to expect God to interfere, even when great evils threaten. The greatest evil, after all, would be that the conditions of genuine character should fail. We come even to rejoice that we live, in this time of our preliminary training, in a world in which the rewards of virtue do not seem to follow either immediately or certainly. The natural and inevitable doubt which underlies for every man "the problem of evil" becomes, in the light of this far reaching principle of reverence for personality, itself a cause of thanksgiving; for it insures that our righteous choices shall not be selfishly motived. We are glad that the genuinely unselfish choice seems so often to cut right athwart our own interests; for it means that our wills are not over-ridden. The very existence of the problem of evil makes possible our belief in the genuineness of the character of ourselves and of others. It is a heavy price that is thus paid, no doubt; but it is not too heavy for the priceless interests so guarded.

We have to recognize, on the part of God, then, something like a really purposed obscuring of the spiritual world. The seeming unreality of the spiritual life is a chief part of our moral and spiritual training.

XXV

OUR VERY QUESTIONINGS A PROOF OF REALITY

But, with reference to all these unremovable causes of the seeming unreality of the spiritual life, we should not fail to notice that our very questionings here are an evidence of reality. It is hard to see how else the questions could arise at all.

In the question of freedom, for example, if the mind were wholly determined, it is difficult to see how the very notion of freedom should arise at all; or if the ideas, which compose it, be conceived somehow to have arisen, it is still more difficult to see how it could mean anything to a mind that did not already know freedom in its own experience. I confess myself quite dissatisfied with the ordinary facile psychological geneses of the conviction of freedom. They seem to me only another great example of the ever-besetting "psychologist's fallacy." The simple fact, that with any intelligence I can raise the question of freedom, that I can give any meaning to it satisfying even to my own mind,—this alone seems to me good evidence of the fact of freedom. The question is itself explicable, only upon the presupposition of the fact.

So, too, in the question of immortality, is not Emerson right in maintaining that the perennial interest with which men perpetually return to this problem, is itself better evidence of the reality of the future life than any proofs which they might discover? If we were mere creatures of the day, complete kindred of animals, it is hard to see how this question of the immortal life should come so to press upon us. Is it not the stirring within us of our own birthright, that prompts the questioning? Is it a false response that men have made, these years since Wordsworth wrote, to his "intimations of immortality"? Are questionings, in truth, no evidence here? Does not, rather, the note of satiety, unrest, disillusion, and final despair, which inevitably shows itself in all poetry that reflects any thorough-going attempt on the part of man to find his entire satisfaction in the flesh, bear unmistakable testimony to the fact that man is more than animal?[1]

So, once more, the very existence of the problem of evil in practically all minds points to its own solution. For the question could not

[1] Cf. Paul E. More: "The Poetry of Arthur Symonds," *The Independent,* April 17, 1902.

arise in all minds, except upon the assumption in all that, in a world that ought to be, happiness and virtue would fall together. But in this common assumption made by all minds, as demanded by their very constitutions, must we not see an unmistakable self-expression of that power that lies back of the universe, and, therefore, an implicit answer to our own doubt,— a virtual pledge that finally, at least, that shall be which is here demanded?

A similar thing is to be said even with reference to the question of the existence and love of God. Unless man is by his very nature religious, it is difficult to see how the primal religious question could even arise. The simple fact that the question is one of never-dying interest to man, that he persistently recurs to it in his highest moments, and unconsciously assumes it in his deepest experiences and even in his commonest activities—the mere fact that he so questions as concerning an absolutely vital interest, is itself strong evidence of the reality of that questioned. Thus "Physicus," in the very act of renouncing all religious faith, says, as if it were a matter of course, "I am confident that truth must in the end be most profitable for the race;" thus unconsciously still betraying a fundamentally religious belief.

Here, too, the persistent, unconscious show-
ings of the nature of men must be taken as self-
expressions of that Absolute which is back of
all, and so evidence of such a God as the soul
seeks. A thoughtful modern novelist thus con-
cludes one of her stories: "Full assurance has
not been granted me, and it is my lot in doing
battle to strike often in the dark. Yet I have
moments when I know that the strife is not in
vain. In these I wonder why we are so troubled
about our duty to our fellow-man, and about
our knowledge of God. The one command in
regard to our neighbor is not obscure. And
our foreboding lest our faith in God shall
escape us seems futile, inasmuch as we cannot
escape from our faith." One can hardly deny
the force of this consideration, without calling
in question that fundamental assumption of all
our thinking and living—the honesty of the
world. When this is denied, all thinking,
scientific, philosophical, or religious, is at an
end.

> "Rather I prize the doubt
> Low kinds exist without,
> Finished and finite clods, untroubled by a spark.
>
> Poor vaunt of life indeed,
> Were man but formed to feed
> On joy, to solely seek and find and feast;
> Such feasting ended, then

As sure an end to men;
Irks care the crop-full bird? Frets doubt the maw-
crammed beast?

Rejoice we are allied
To That which doth provide
And not partake, effect and not receive!
A spark disturbs our clod;
Nearer we hold of God
Who gives, than of his tribes that take, I must believe.

Then, welcome each rebuff
That turns earth's smoothness rough,
Each sting that bids nor sit nor stand, but go!
Be our joys three parts pain!
Strive, and hold cheap the strain;
Learn, nor account the pang; dare, never grudge the throe!

For thence—a paradox
Which comforts while it mocks—
Shall life succeed in that it seems to fail:
What I aspired to be,
And was not, comforts me:
A brute I might have been, but would not sink i' the
scale."

PART II
THE WAY INTO REALITY

THE PRESUMPTIVE EVIDENCE

XXVI

THE TEST OF PRESENT TRENDS OF THOUGHT—HISTORICAL, PHILOSOPHICAL, SCIENTIFIC, ETHICAL, AND SOCIAL

We shall do well to preface our positive discussion of the way into reality in religious thought and life by a brief but comprehensive survey of the presumptive evidence of the reality and significance of the spiritual life, in view of its connections with the great present trends of thought, and in view of the inevitably fundamental nature of religion.

If the spiritual life is to become for us an assured and significant reality, it must seem to us, as we have seen, both to be inextricably knit up with all else that we count most real, and also to have its own distinct and valuable contribution to make to life. Both things must be true, if the spiritual life is to become for us of fundamental importance. This chapter and the next are devoted to showing briefly how Christianity meets the first demand,—to pointing out the indissoluble connection of the Christian thought and life with the realest trends of our own times.

If one thinks, then, of those trends of thought which are realest for our own time, and seeks to test the spiritual life by them, he would probably have to say: that first, religion must meet the test of psychology; secondly, the test of a social, and therefore an ethical consciousness; and that would mean, in the third place, that the spiritual life must be fully awake to the reality and meaning of the personal; fourth, it must possess a scientific sense of law and unity; and, finally, it must be able, as well, to meet the historical and philosophical test.

The limits of this book do not permit a full treatment of any of these different tests; but we may consider briefly, in reverse order, their application to Christianity.

Christianity, then, may not shrink from either a historical or philosophical investigation. Least of all, in a scientific age, can it claim the right to withdraw itself from the testing of long experience. And the Christian religion can retain for the modern man its full significance only if it can meet just this test. And, in the same way, if a careful historical study of Christianity, as it manifests itself in the life of the race, side by side with other religions, does not prove the superiority of Christianity, its supreme claims cannot seem to us ultimately justified. Inevitably, whether it will or not, every religion is steadily undergoing such a test, and is being tried out by a relentless application of the principle of the survival of the fittest. It is hardly open to doubt, that, so tested, the teaching, ideals, and religion of Jesus verify themselves to an extent scarcely approached by any other point of view.

In a similar sense, Christianity cannot withdraw itself from philosophical investigation. However great may be one's sympathy with many of Ritschl's positives, the thoughtful man can hardly deny the justice of Dr. Bruce's criticism of Ritschl because of his refusal to recognize that philosophy has any legitimate task in the realm of religion. As Dr. Bruce says: "The horror of metaphysics is a reaction to be transcended." "The Christian religion *implies* a theory of the universe." "If Christ's doctrine is true, there ought to be something in the world to verify it." Quite in harmony with this criticism, was Professor Everett's belief that the mistake of the Ritschlians lay in separating wholly from philosophy, from the great movements of history, and from natural religion.

There are plain dangers, then, in a view that tries to withdraw Christianity from the philosophical test. First, there is the danger of failing to see that one may so over-emphasize the uniqueness of the revelation of God in Christ, as to take it out of its connection with all other reality, and so tend to make it unreal. A second danger is that of underestimating the revelation of God in our own natures. These, too, we may not forget, are, upon any sane view, from God,—the same God who has revealed himself in Christ. There will probably be some indication of this identity of origin. Christianity must fit human nature and the whole man. And the way in which Christianity fits man must finally be regarded as its greatest proof, and must even underlie our belief in Christ himself.

Still another danger of such a view is that it should fail to see the necessity of a unified Christian view of the world. If the Christian is to be at the same time a thinker, he cannot avoid the attempt to bring the different sides of his experience into relation to each other, and into a final unity. It is quite true that this philosophical attempt is not the introduction to religion, and is not its foundation; but it is a needed supplement for, at least, the intellectual peace of even the individual Christian soul. And so long as this need of an ultimate unity is not met, the Christian religion must still seem in some degree irrational and unreal; for it will not seem to one to fit the world as he finds it.

The believer in the Christian thought and life, therefore, if he sees things aright, must himself desire that philosophy should freely apply its own tests to Christianity, though he may have a clear sense that the philosophical consideration must at best be no adequate measure of the whole significance of religion. The most direct proof that Christianity does not fail to meet the test of the best philosophical thought of our time is found, perhaps, in the general acceptance of the Christian ethical ideal, and in the predominant ethical note of our ablest philosophical thinkers, and the way in which they make even metaphysics root in ethics. The significance, even for philosophy, of the great personalities of history is also a growing conviction.

So, too, it is quite impossible for one to belong to the present generation and not demand that religion shall show, from the scientific point of view, some *sense of law and unity* in the spiritual life. This will mean, no doubt, on the one hand, the growing recognition of the immanence of God, and, on the other hand, the perception that the laws of the spiritual world are

chiefly the laws of personal relations. On the
one hand, then, as Professor Coe has said,[1] "the
sense of a divine presence can and does pene-
trate all human faculties. It is not limited to
special occasions, or to moments of exaltation.
. . . . In a word, the religious experience is
what we should expect it to be if the doctrine
of the immanence of God is true." And, on the
other hand, if the spiritual life is the highest
life of spirits, of persons, then its fundamental
laws, it would seem, must be the laws of deepening personal relations with men and with God.
Subsidiary laws, doubtless, there will be, but
all closely related to these fundamental laws.
Christianity is quite able to meet this scientific
demand. Indeed, science's assertion of the universality of law is only a "disguised expression"
for the final Unity of things, so strongly asserted
by a theistic view. And the more surely the
Christian believes in a "faithful Creator," the
more surely will he rest in the great recognized
laws of the spiritual, as well as the material
world.

And, again, for a generation to which the *personal* means more than to any that has preceded,
religion must be peculiarly marked with a
sense of the value and sacredness of the person.

[1] *The Religion of a Mature Mind,* pp. 342-343.

And this sense can hardly fail to dominate any theology that is to meet the deeper demand of our times.

In a precisely similar way, our conception of religion must meet the very marked *social and ethical consciousness* of our time. When one tries to see exactly what the social consciousness involves, it will be found to include the sense of the fundamental likeness of men, of their inevitable mutual influence, of the value and sacredness of the individual person, as well as the sense of obligation to others, and love. The very statement of these elements of the social consciousness suggests how surely akin they are to the demands of the Christian spirit, how certainly, indeed, they have grown naturally out of Christ's conception of every man as a child of God. And that "rational ethical democracy," to which the social evolution looks, is hardly other than the "civilization of brotherly men" of the Kingdom of God.[1]

[1] For the detailed argument cf. King: *Theology and the Social Consciousness,* Chapters V-XII.

XXVII

THE TEST OF PRESENT TRENDS OF THOUGHT—PSYCHOLOGICAL

It may be worth while to pause a little longer upon the psychological test of the Christian religion. For in this psychological test are involved, in a kind of concrete way, all the other tests. And it can hardly fail to be suggestive to try to apply to the Christian view and life the test of the four great inferences of modern psychology, once before used to suggest the great common conditions of all the activities of our life: the complexity of life, the unity of the mind, the central importance of will and action, and the concreteness of the real.

Does Christianity, conceived as life, meet these tests? The recognition of the *complexity of life* on the part of Christianity seems to me to be clearly shown in the fact that Christianity is, in the first place, not ascetic. My own clear judgment is in entire agreement with that of Professor James Seth that Christ's conception cannot be regarded as truly ascetic, in the ordinary acceptance of that term.[1] Christ certainly

[1] *Rational Living*, pp. 93-102; cf. James Seth: "On certain Alleged Defects in Christian Morality," *Hibbert Journal,* October, 1907.

neither lives nor thinks as an ascetic. His whole
point of view is rather that of recognizing all
life as coming from the Father, and all its goods
to be rejoiced in as goods; though with distinct
recognition that some are inferior to others, and
that, if need be, the lower must be unhesitatingly sacrificed to the higher.

The similar refusal of the whole New Testament to draw any line of separation between the
sacred and the secular, is another proof of Christianity's recognition of the complexity of life.
Christianity's knitting up of the human and the
divine, too, is itself an assertion of the same fact.
The Christian view is no gnosticism. God is
for it the source of all. And it is the same God,
that made the world and man, who reveals himself in Christ. The very assertion of the incar-
nation, and the conception of duty as the will of
God, of love as the first and great commandment, and of God himself as love and personal,
are all so many separate assertions of the complexity and interrelatedness of all life. And in
this growing psychological conviction of the
complexity of life, of the interrelatedness of all,
we are, thus, only returning to the standpoint
of Christ and of the New Testament.

And so harmonious is the teaching of Jesus
with the present psychological emphasis upon

the *unity of mind,* that this may even be called one of the four fundamental principles and motives chiefly used by Christ in the Sermon on the Mount. He appeals repeatedly to the principle of the unity of the spiritual life, insisting that it is impossible to fall below one's best at one point and be all that one ought to be at other points. And it is hardly too much to say that, in its recognition of the unity of the mind, the Christian conception fulfils most completely both the intellectual and the emotional conditions of rational living.

On the intellectual side, it gives the most needed helps, and is able to face the most dangerous hindrances.

While it makes no attempt to answer all curious intellectual inquiries, it does give, in the great revelation in Christ, sufficient ground for faith. The history of the Christian world is itself the best proof that beyond any other influence, it has also brought men to full self-consciousness.

At the same time, as Romanes so suggestively says, it has left men free for all scientific inquiry. "One of the strongest pieces of objective evidence," he says, "in favor of Christianity . . . . is the absence from the biography of Christ of any doctrine which the subsequent growth of human knowledge—whether in natural science, ethics, political economy, or elsewhere—has had to discount. This negative argument is really almost as strong as is the positive one from what Christ did teach. For, when we consider what a large number of sayings are recorded of—or at least attributed to—him, it becomes most remarkable that in literal truth there is no reason why any of his words should ever pass away in the sense of becoming obsolete. 'Not even now could it be easy,' says John Stuart Mill, 'even for an unbeliever, to find a better translation of the rule of virtue from the abstract into the concrete, than to endeavor so to live that Christ would approve our life.' Contrast Jesus Christ in this respect with other thinkers of like antiquity. Even Plato, who though some four hundred years before Christ in point of time, was greatly in advance of him in respect of philosophic thought—not only because Athens then presented the extraordinary phenomenon which it did of genius in all directions never since equalled, but also because he, following Socrates, was, so to speak, the greatest representative of human reason in the direction of spirituality—even Plato, I say, is nowhere in this respect as compared with Christ. Read the dialogues, and see how enormous is the contrast with the Gospels in respect of errors of all kinds —reaching even to absurdity in respect to reason, and to sayings shocking to the moral sense. Yet this is confessedly the highest level of human reason on the lines of spirituality, when unaided by alleged revelation."

And the contribution which Christianity makes even on the intellectual side, in that it gives a clear, definite, ethical ideal in Christ, is quite inestimable. The intellectual stimulus of such an ideal, to say nothing of its moral value, is beyond computation.

And when one thinks of the chief intellectual hindrances in true living—over-sophistication, making insights take the place of doing, and intellectual vagueness—it can hardly be doubted that Christianity is peculiarly adapted to meet them. In its firm hold, through Christ, on great convictions and ideals, it has no room for sophistication; and its predominant moral interest and insistent ethical demand definitely shut out those who hear and do not. At the same time, both the definiteness of Christ's ethical ideals and his conception of all moral demands as the will of a loving Father, stand opposed to the greatest dangers of intellectual vagueness.

In the same way, too, the example and the teaching of Christ point to the best and most normal emotional conditions. If we really believe the teaching of Jesus, there is already open to us the most ideal emotional conditions for the highest living. It cannot fail to give what psychology recognizes as the stimulating effect of joyful emotions. It is truly a religion of good tidings. With its trust in a loving Father and its conception of all duty as his will, its view of life as training, and its assurance of the immortal hope, it brings to men all of good that a religion can well be conceived to bring.

Putting men, as it does, face to face with an incomparable literary and personal expression of the greatest truths and motives, it calls out in men, too, in the profoundest way, the needed sober and strenuous moods for the highest willing. Christianity is equally decisive in setting aside all strained and sham and passive emotions. Neither in Christ's example nor in his teaching is stress anywhere laid on feeling. It is rather taken as an incidental result of true living. And in its powerful and combined appeal to reason and conscience and will, it gives power to suspend action in the face of strong emotion. Christianity never allows the right of simple feeling to rule.

Just because it is profoundly ethical, Christianity cannot fail to recognize, with modern

12

psychology, *the enormous place of will in life.*
It is only in that ethical living that takes place
in personal relations, that the whole will is
called out. And in this stimulating and strength-
ening of the will, Christianity has at the same
time, in accordance with this psychological emphasis, strengthened and deepened all the life of
men. It has made men capable of being more,
of counting more, of enjoying more. So, too,
psychology's recognition of the fundamental
nature of self-control may be regarded as dis-
tinctively Christian. Indeed, Christ's great,
fundamental, all-inclusive law of losing the life
to save the life is only the highest expression
of self-control. And Christianity's ethical demand, once more, calls for self-control so constantly that its attitude has even been mistaken
for that of asceticism. Moreover, the self-
control which Christianity enjoins and makes
possible is not merely negative, but thoroughly
positive, as psychology demands that it should
be.

And Christianity meets in an even deeper
way the insistence of psychology on the central
importance of will and action, by the thorough-
going fashion in which it makes the objective
mood—the mood of activity and of work—
the normal mood of man. In a degree true

of no other influence, it has proved able to
take men out of themselves, in its absorption
of them in the great work of a great cause, and
in the great love of a great Saviour. In this
very way it not only fulfils for men a chief
condition of character and happiness and influence, but it brings to them a chief means of
all three, in work which can be the fullest expression of man's best self; work that men can
think of as God-given, and, because service both
to God and to men, as of abiding worth. Christianity calls men even to the sharing of Christ's
own vicarious and redemptive work.

And finally, Christianity exemplifies not less
fully psychology's fourth fundamental insistence on the *concreteness of the real,* in its preëminent respect for the person—the greatest
condition of character and happiness and influence, and in its preëminent use of personal
association—the greatest means to character and
happiness and influence. For the assertion of
the concreteness of the real is finally the insistence upon the personal in the whole of its
range. Now, on the one hand, respect for the
person lies so deeply imbedded in the very
spirit of Christianity, that one cannot fail to
see it in the entire conduct and teaching of
Jesus. One cannot fail to regard it, according

to the Christian conception, as even the fundamental principle of God in his treatment of men; and he cannot doubt, as Lotze and Wundt have both borne testimony, that to Christianity it is due that this respect for man as man has come into the world. On the other hand, the very fact that Christianity points not to a redeeming doctrine, but to a redeeming person, and professes to open to men a constant, intimate, and unobtrusive relation of the personal Spirit of God with their spirits, shows how firmly imbedded in the Christian teaching is the thought of the supreme importance of personal association.

With even so rapid and imperfect an attempt to apply to Christianity the tests of modern psychology, one can hardly fail to see that here at least the Christian view is indubitably connected with one of the realest trends of our own time, and meets with convincing satisfaction all the tests involved in the dominant elements of this trend.

XXVIII

MAN'S ESSENTIAL NEED OF RELIGION

But in order that the spiritual life might become to us most real and significant, we found not only that it must be connected indubitably with all that is realest to us, but must also be seen to make its own unmistakable and indispensable contribution to life. That is, we must be not only radically liberal in our view in the recognition of the inter-relatedness of religion with all life, but also radically Christian in the recognition of the essential and unique contribution of religion itself.

That religion has most assuredly this contribution to make, no man can doubt, who has once caught a glimpse of the fundamental nature of religion. For myself, this comes out most clearly in seeing how inevitably, as I have elsewhere pointed out, a faith essentially religious logically underlies all our reasoning, all work worth doing, all strenuous moral endeavor, all earnest social service. The argument so closely concerns the present inquiry that its reproduction here may be pardoned.

For, in the first place, a faith essentially religious logically underlies *all our reasoning*. For every argument that we can possibly make, especially concerning any of the greater interests of life, must go forward upon the double assumption of the consistency and the worth of the world. We can reason at all, only so far as we have already virtually asserted that the world is a world in which we can rationally *think;* and our most significant arguments require, as well, that we should add the faith that the world is a world in which we can rationally *live.* That, in other words, there is the unity and consistency of one truth and of a unified reason in the world, and an essential love at its heart that makes life abundantly worth living. And these two fundamental assumptions of all our reasoning are essentially religious convictions.

That men often do not recognize these logical implications of their reasoning, and may use with great complacency impersonal and irreligious language concerning their experience that will not bear thinking through—this is all too true; but this does not alter the fact of the ultimate logical implications of their deepest thinking and living. The mere report, therefore, of the psychological facts of a man's religious experience, as he conceives it, is by no means the final step in any fundamental religious inquiry.

In the same way, a faith essentially religious

underlies *all work worth doing*. For, as Paulsen
says, speaking simply as a philosopher, 'Who-
ever devotes his life to a cause believes in that
cause; and this belief, be his creed what it
may, has always something of the form of religion.' 'Hence,' he adds, 'faith infers that an
inner connection exists between the real and
the valuable within the domain of history, and
believes that in history something like an im-
manent principle of reason or justice favors
the right and the good and leads it to victory
over all resisting forces.' It is impossible, that
is, for a man with full consciousness to throw
himself enthusiastically into a work which he
regards from the start as absolutely hopeless.
When, then, he takes up the work of his life calling, or the cause to which he devotes himself, as
work really worth while, in which he can lose
himself with joy, whether consciously or not,
he is virtually asserting his faith in a plan larger
than his own plan, the all-embracing plan of
the on-going providence of God, which shall
catch up the little fragments of his work into
a larger whole and make them contribute, thus,
to a goal greater than any that the man himself
may set. To believe in the final worth of one's
own work, then, logically implies a real belief
in God. For 'principles' and 'plans' and 'laws,'
so far as I am able to see, have no real existence,
that will bear thorough thinking, and can *do*
nothing, apart from a Being that must be conceived ultimately in essentially personal terms.

A fully religious conviction logically underlies all enthusiastic work.

In *all strenuous moral endeavor,* in the fight for character for one's self, a faith essentially religious is in like manner involved. So Martineau asserts: 'Nothing less than the majesty of God, and the power of the world to come, can maintain the peace and sanctity of our homes, the order and serenity of our minds, the spirit of patience and tender mercy in our hearts.' For here, once more, we shall not earnestly attempt a hopeless task. And if, in the surrender to the highest in us, we cannot believe that we thereby at the same time link ourselves to the highest in the universe, we shall not be able to reach that courage which gives promise of any high attainment. Only the highest motives are finally sufficient here. If our faith in the ultimate ethical trend of the great power back of the universe really breaks down, we shall hardly be able to keep our faith even in our own ideals.

That this faith in the ethical trend of the universe is always consciously present, or even the need of it definitely felt in any recognized religious way, I am far from affirming. . . . . There are great temperamental differences here, doubtless, and the very force of life in us may carry us over many thin places in our reasoning, without misgiving; but the fact remains that hopeful, courageous, moral endeavor logically requires the faith that we are not here at war with the ultimate purpose of things.

And, once more, a faith essentially religious logically underlies, in like manner, *all earnest social service*. I do not forget that in the inconsistency of our natures men may often go on in forgetfulness of the real significance of their actions, and in the strength of motives which they have at least formally denied. Nor do I forget that it is possible for social service itself to become, for the time being, even a kind of fad, and for the phrases of the new social consciousness of our time to become only a new cant. Nor do I forget that men in such unselfish service may honestly think of themselves, for a time, as not needing in any degree either the convictions or the consolations of religion.

Nevertheless, when I try really to think the situation through, I am not able to doubt that Nash is right when he says: 'Nothing save a settled and fervid conviction that the universe is on the side of the will . . . . can give the will the force and edge suitable.' For here, also, we shall not throw ourselves with all abandon into a task that we think either hopeless or worthless. And that means that we must have back of our social service the great religious convictions of the love of God and the worth of men. We shall not attempt to dip out the ocean with a cup, and we shall not enter on a boundless social task in which there is no hope of accomplishing any permanent and large result. We *must* believe here that we work with God, in line with his own purpose, and that the mighty will of the living God is pledged to our attempt.[1]

Moreover, let it here be added, so far as the Christian religion is able to fulfil its promise of putting men into real communion with God known as Father; so far as it is able to give undoubted worth to life in the conception of man as child of God; so long as it can find in all duty simply the will of a loving Father; and so long as it can give to men assured faith in an immortal life of most significant work and of the highest personal association—so long must Christianity have an indispensable contribution to make to human life. A truly Christian faith can alone give the ideal conditions of the richest life.

If we turn, now, from this general consideration of the presumptive evidence of the reality and significance of the spiritual life, to seek to indicate more definitely just how we are to find our way into reality here, we may well raise three questions: How may we proceed most positively and satisfactorily in our rational argument for the existence of a God who truly fulfils the Christian conception? How are we to find our way into an undoubted personal relation to God? How is reality to be brought

[1] *Personal and Ideal Elements in Education*, pp. 90-97.

into single Christian doctrines? That is, what is the way into the reality of the spiritual life, as to the theistic argument, as to personal relation to God, and as to particular Christian doctrines?

AS TO THE THEISTIC ARGUMENT

XXIX

FACING THE FACTS OFTEN IGNORED

The inquiry into the causes of the seeming unreality of the spiritual world is fundamental. Unless it is thoroughly made, no attempted positive argument can satisfy. But, on the other hand, this inquiry cannot be thoroughly made, as we have seen, without really involving at numerous points some indication of the positive way out. For the very reason, therefore, that we have dwelt so long on the reasons for the seeming obscurity of spiritual truth and life, and upon the presumptive evidence of the reality of the spiritual, we may hope to state with brevity and yet with explicitness our positive conclusions, making use at every point of results already reached.

It is worth remembering, as well, that, in any case, our positions on really ultimate questions are best determined by broad considerations rather than by minute argumentation. We legitimately set aside great masses of such minute argumentation when it is seen to proceed from a point of view, on good grounds rejected by us. One sometimes feels that one of the main rewards of the experience of living is to be found in just this acquired ease in calmly setting aside great piles of logic, that have gone forward upon some large gratuitous assumption, or that have quite left out of account the main consideration. One is sometimes asked what he does with such and such a line of argument. Well, when a man has definitely abandoned on good grounds a given standpoint, he doesn't do anything with the massive arguments which proceed from that standpoint.

And in reaching decisive points of view, it is particularly enlightening to see how very simple and brief the dominating considerations in one's mind have been. You can read no strong, thinking man at length, still less get into intimate conversation with him, without finding, if you refuse to be confused by the mere multiplicity of words, that there are in him a few absolutely dominant convictions capable of very brief and simple statement, and in fact only capable, in themselves, of such statement. Three or four sentences may contain the heart of the man's whole argument for some fundamental position.

These facts are particularly worth recalling in connection with this question of religious conviction and life; for let us frankly say that the decisive, positive considerations here—the considerations that really determine—probably can be put with surprising brevity. It is not necessarily a matter of tomes. Indeed, one may well wonder whether the real grounds of our convictions have not been greatly obscured by many of these elaborate argumentations for God.

I turn, then, with some hope, to attempt, in the light of the principles already reached, a comparatively brief statement, both of the theistic argument and of our personal relation to God.

And, as to the theistic argument, we seem to need, first, definitely to face the facts ignored by the various misconceptions and mistaken or inadequate points of view, which have given the sense of unreality to the spiritual life; and, so, to see the thoroughly fundamental nature of the theistic position; and thus to reach the main possible lines of the theistic argument.

To begin with, we cannot expect sound results without definitely facing and taking into full account the facts ignored in the various mistaken views of the spiritual life that have been considered. This, we have seen, involves, first, some adequate recognition of the great common conditions of life, bodily and psychical—conditions that continually affect our thinking as well as our living. In particular, for our religious thinking, we found that that meant that we must bear in mind the practical nature of all knowledge and belief: that knowledge is never a merely passive process, and that no merely theoretical solution of our problem is possible. This compelled us to set aside as impossible, or unreasonable, in religious thinking, mathematical demonstration, overwhelming evidence, any substitute for living experience, the expectation of meeting difficulties out of hand, taking up the religious inquiry as something wholly new, overrating single intellectual difficulties and negative criticism, forgetting the results of long ignoring of facts, and especially forgetting the ideal assumptions which underlie all our practical beliefs.

To face the facts ignored in the mistaken views of the spiritual life meant also, we found, definite guarding against the common fallacies of ignoring all that cannot be precisely formulated, of making the intellectual the sole standard of reality, and of being dominated by a word, by an analogy, or by the merely imageable.

Sound theistic thinking, we saw, further, required that we should set aside as quite unwarranted certain traditional objections: both those which come from an undue exaltation of the mathematico-mechanical view of the world—

like the difficulties of an abstract intellectualism, of a crude sensationalism, or of an impossible hypostasizing of laws; and those philosophical difficulties which are supposed to put religion at peculiar disadvantage. Here we found that religion had no peculiar responsibility for the solution of epistemological and metaphysical problems; that the doctrine of the relativity of knowledge did not concern it in any special way; that, in particular, the terms "Absolute" and "Unchangeable," as applied to God, were not to be gratuitously taken as putting God out of all real touch with men; that "Infinite" and "Personality" could by no means be taken as terms mutually contradictory; and that, rather, the attempted impersonal conceptions of God were the conceptions that refused to resolve into any clear meaning.

We have seen, also, as bearing on the problem of thorough-going religious thinking, that the religious problem must be in certain points clearly distinguished from both the scientific and philosophical problems. From the scientific problem: as a problem of ideal interpretation rather than of causal connection; a problem of ultimate inference, rather than of merely phenomenal inquiry; as attempting a different ideal construction of the world from that attempted by science; and as requiring the whole man in a way not true of the scientific problem, which is, far more truly, purely intellectual.

From the philosophical problem as ordinarily conceived, the problem of ultimate religious thinking was differentiated as definitely bringing into its inferences as data the facts of the historical revelation of God,—the preëminent spiritual facts of the race. And it was insisted that we had no right to expect a complete solution from an investigation that ignored these most important data of all.

The sense of unreality of the spiritual life which comes from failure to fulfil the natural conditions, concerns theistic thinking only indirectly, yet very really. For these conditions point out the one way to that experience of the spiritual life, which alone can give the key to any adequate interpretation of that life, and to any really decisive thinking concerning it. This is simply the common-sense requirement that a man should know something of what he is talking about.

So far, in our summary of the facts to be faced by theistic thinking, we have dealt with what we have called the removable causes of the seeming unreality of the spiritual life.

When we ask as to the bearing upon our religious thinking of the unremovable causes, we find ourselves obliged to take clear account of the limitations and fluctuations of our finite natures. We have, then, to recognize that our view of the world is necessarily partial; that by our very natures we are discursive in our living and thinking; that we are obliged to reckon upon a certain ebb and flow in our sense of reality everywhere; that we must expect these limitations and fluctuations to be specially felt in the religious inquiry, where we are dealing with the problems of the Infinite, where the grounds of our convictions lie quite below the surface, and where so much depends upon the ethical attitude. In view of this inevitable fluctuation in the sense of reality, we saw that we must give special importance to the witness of our consciously best hours.

The further thought—that this seeming unreality is in part definitely intended for our better moral and spiritual training—suggests, in spite of great similarities, that there is a reason that must be decisive in any question of the spiritual life, why we should not expect here even such proof as might be readily accessible in other spheres of life. God is moved, in this hiding of himself, by an abiding reverence for our human individuality and moral initiative. And yet, even in this intended obscurity, we found an implied evidence. Our very questionings, to be themselves explicable, seemed necessarily a proof of that about which they questioned.

This bare summary, perhaps, justifies the conclusion that there are here considerations which have an important bearing on all theistic thinking, and that our theistic argument must go forward in clear recognition of these considerations. In particular, we have felt that these considerations gave reasonable ground for setting aside initial objections to the theistic argument, and for meeting some of the most important difficulties both as to the conception of God, and as to the relation of God to the finite. At the same time they have brought clearly into view the necessary limitations in such theistic proofs as may be attempted. We seem prepared, thus, to pass to a brief and comprehensive statement of the main lines of the theistic argument; although it may be doubted whether, when one has given full weight to the considerations just reviewed, the mere formulation of the theistic argument has much contribution to make.

XXX

THE NECESSARY LIMITATIONS IN THE ARGUMENT

And, first, let us definitely state, in the light of the principles already traversed, the necessary limitations in the theistic argument. From our present position, we can see beforehand, that no strict and demonstrative proof of the existence of God is possible. We shall not be surprised, therefore, at the manifest limitations of the ordinary forms of the theistic argument. Many things forbid anything like strict proof here.

In the first place, there is no absolute demonstration outside of mathematics, but only probable reasoning. A strict mathematical demonstration, then, is here impossible.

Moreover, even in the only sense in which we may speak of strict proof outside of mathematics—the case of complete deduction—it cannot be applied to God. For, as Purinton has pointed out, such deduction involves a classing of the individual concerning whom the argument is made, and God admits of no such classing. He is not one of a class of gods. A strict deductive argument, also, is, then, impossible.

Moreover, if one attempts to reach his conclusion by induction, it is plain that we can know, and have to do, only with finite data. Now, it cannot be that finite data should give us sufficient ground for a strict inference to the Infinite. A strict inductive proof is thus impossible.

Once more, if one is to use terms with full accuracy, the actual concrete in any case cannot be reached in a demonstrative way. We can only know the concrete—a Person, in this case—in experience; and, in the present argument, there is the further difficulty, that God is not for us a direct sensuous fact; and, moreover, in the nature of the case, any manifestation of him, that we could take in, must be necessarily finite. His fulness could only be partly manifested. Along the line, then, of even some kind of perception, an Infinite could not be strictly given.

Again, the moral reasons for the comparative hiddenness of God have to be considered—both that sense of the unreality of God which comes from long practical ignoring of him, and that intended unobtrusiveness of God which arises from his reverent regard for the human personality. In such a situation, also, strict proof is plainly set aside. The moral argument cannot be made coercive.

Finally, strict proof here is impossible, because that which is to be the goal of the argument for God, must be really the fundamental assumption of *all* argument, including that made for God. This will be more clear later. We may content ourselves now with Lotze's statement that all these proofs for the existence of God themselves "presuppose the absolute validity of a truth which knits all the world together," and so seem in part, at least, to assume at the start their conclusion. The difficulty is not unlike that in which any argument for the trustworthiness of our faculties is involved, where, as we have seen, it is evident that, if any weight is to be given to the argument, one must assume the trustworthiness of the faculties which make the argument, but which by hypothesis are under question. So, as to the argument for God, just so far as the goal is assumed in the argument, it is plainly not strictly proved.

There seem, then, to be decisive reasons why a strict proof, in any sense, of the existence of God is not to be expected. What lines of argument are open?

XXXI

THE MAIN LINES OF ARGUMENT

It should be remembered that we are here speaking of argument, not of life-experience.

We may argue, first, directly from the fact of Christ himself,—his life, his teaching, and especially his consciousness—as the greatest and most significant fact in the world, and so our best proof of the existence of God in the full Christian sense. This seems to me, even from the side of pure argument, the most decisive proof. The argument goes upon the simple assumption that, if we are ever to discern the real nature of the ultimate world-ground, our best light must come from the greatest and most significant facts. For myself, I have no doubt that Christ is the most significant of all facts known to us, and, therefore, the best basis for direct and decisive inference to the nature of the world-ground. The argument does not at all go, it should be noticed, upon any assumption of the arbitrary authority of Jesus, but simply upon the significance of what he is. Any authority subsequently given him must be based wholly upon what he is in fact found to be. I count the fact of Christ, the greatest of all proofs of a completely satisfying God,—the proof most powerful to produce conviction in the mind of a man who has himself come to full moral self-consciousness.

One may argue, similarly, (but less decisively, so long as Christ is omitted) from the whole historical revelation of God—from the line of the prophets, and from the great spiritual seers of all time, as constituting the greatest and most significant historical movement of the world. Persons are incontrovertibly the greatest facts, and the most significant data. Let us not, then, ignore the most decisive evidences in our search for God, nor underestimate the greatness of the personalities with whom we have here to do. One may well recall the words of a thorough-going modern critic like Cornill, concerning Amos and Hosea, for example. "Amos," he says, "is one of the most marvellous and in-comprehensible figures in the history of the human mind, the pioneer of a process of evo-lution, from which a new epoch of humanity dates." And Hosea, too, he counts "among the greatest religious geniuses which the world has ever produced."[1] We are not to suppose that the argument from such personalities is less

---

[1] *The Prophets*, pp. 46, 50.

significant than the argument from things. God is best known in his completest manifestations.

Turning to lines of argument more traditional, it may be justly urged that the plain logical defects to be pointed out in all the common forms of the cosmological, teleological, and ontological proofs, seem themselves to show a practical initial certainty of God, on other grounds. These arguments have been taken as sufficiently satisfying, and not narrowly scrutinized, because their goal was really assumed to be already certain. It is very difficult to explain, otherwise, the weight that has actually been attached to arguments, which in strict logical form are quite inconclusive. We have seen why they could not be conclusive; we are here simply trying to face the question: Why are they felt to be still so satisfying, though so strictly inconclusive? The natural answer is, the goal of the argument is practically taken by us all as an immediate certainty. A quite insufficient proof satisfies our intellectual conscience, simply because we are already sure of the conclusion.

This brings us to a fourth suggested line of argument. Our only possible standard of truth is in our own constitution. In consequence, all proof of every kind moves on a double assumption: first, that the world is a sphere of rational thinking—must satisfy the intellect; second, that the world is a sphere of rational living—must satisfy the whole man. One might say that this double assumption is the heart of the intention of the ontological argument, and suggests the two forms in which that argument may be stated, or the double interpretation of our necessary constant assumption that the world is a "rational," or an "honest" world.

The Hegelian form of the argument—"the real is rational"—starts from the intellectual demand of our natures; has for its test of truth, logical consistency; and affirms the rationality of the world in the simply intellectual sense, and so finds the world a sphere for rational *thinking*. This form of the argument asserts that the world must be thinkable, intelligible. It is by no means able to prove this universal assertion; but it simply points out that every bit of thinking, every single argument, must really assume for its own justification the rationality—the honesty—of the world in this sense.

What, perhaps, may be called the Lotzian form of the argument—"that which is most worthy must exist"—starts from the side of our interests, from a judgment of worth—an essentially ethical judgment; it has for its test of truth, worth; and affirms the rationality of the world not in the narrower, merely intellectual sense, but in the broad sense, as satisfying the whole man; and it, thus, finds the world a sphere for rational *living*. It holds, that is, as an immediate conviction, that the world must be not merely construable, thinkable to the understanding as a chain of causes and effects, but a world in which we can live, and in which we can cherish our ideals—a world that can satisfy the whole man. Paulsen thus states the position: "I could not live, I could not breathe and move freely in a world that is nothing but an enormous, senseless, and soulless machine; hence I cannot believe that it is such a machine; hence I believe that it is the revelation of an all-wise and all-good God, even though my eyes fail to see him and my understanding comprehend him not."[1] A completely rational world, it is here asserted, must have value, must go back to a purpose of good. It must be worth while. It must not play fast and loose with me. Otherwise, I am left at cross-purposes with myself; my ethical and æsthetic demands are all unmet; the world is for me an intolerable world.

We are scarcely aware to what an extent this assumption permeates all our reasoning on ques-

[1] *Introduction to Philosophy*, p. 420.

tions in any degree moral and spiritual. All the arguments that really weigh with us to-day, for freedom, and for immortality, for example, go forward on the plainly implied major premise that the world is not absurd and intolerable. So James says as to freedom: "The whole feeling of reality, the whole sting and excitement of our voluntary life, depends on our sense that in it things are *really being decided* from one moment to another, and that it is not the dull rattling off of a chain that was forged innumerable ages ago."[2]   And he cannot persuade himself that this feeling, which alone gives reality and meaning to life, can be a mere illusion. Tennyson's argument as to immortality goes forward upon a precisely similar assumption:

> "My own dim life should teach me this,
>   That life shall live forevermore,
>   Else earth is darkness at the core,
> And dust and ashes all that is."

He cannot believe that this awful alternative is possible.

Underlying, then, all our rational living, all setting of goals we count worthy, all thinking, even, concerning the life of the *whole* man, is the initial assumption that the world is rational

[2] *Psychology*, Briefer Course, p. 237.

in the broadest sense, that that which ought to be is, that Living Love is the source of all.

Now it should be noted, neither of these two assumptions, involved in the assertion of the rationality or honesty of the world, can be fully met and made thinkable, except by the existence of a living, personal, loving God, whose reason and whose love are in truth the sure basis of all our thinking and living. The so-called eternal truths, logical or ethical, can have no existence and power of their own; they are finally intelligible only when conceived as the actual modes of activity of God himself. No argument of any kind for anything can be framed that does not in some way virtually make these assumptions of the reason and love of God. The real truth, therefore, concerning all our theistic arguments seems to be this: they do not reach their goal at all, except upon an assumption that implies that the goal has been already reached in immediate conviction. It is for just this reason that we are comparatively unaffected by their logical defects.

To see, now, the fundamental nature of these two great assumptions that underlie all our thinking and living, is really to see that the existence of a God of reason and love is so certain and fundamental a fact, that it really

has to be assumed in all thinking and living—
a fact that cannot be proved just because it is
the basis of all proof;—the postulate, without
which we should ultimately be driven to give
up altogether the possibility of rational thinking.
And we need to remind ourselves how often, in
both scientific and philosophical questions, when
we try to think our terms and conceptions completely through, we are driven necessarily beyond the finite, if we are to avoid plain self-
contradiction.   We cannot think the finite as
simply finite.   The real reality, as Bradley
points out, which persistently forces itself upon
us in intellectual thinking, is a reality absolutely
consistent and all-embracing.   Even science cannot finally do without such a basis, as Spencer's
so-called Unknowable testifies.

An additional reason is thus given us, why to
our ordinary thinking God should seem peculiarly hidden, and his existence not easily shown.
He cannot be proved, because his existence is
necessarily assumed in all proof.   Along with
the clear perception of the inevitable limitations
of the theistic arguments, therefore, the thoroughly fundamental nature of the theistic
position is at the same time shown.   It is so
fundamental, that to relinquish it is to relinquish
all hope of rationality in any part of our final

14

thinking, and, indeed, to surrender the logical
bases of all thinking and living. The religious
postulate, thus, is necessary to all the rest of life.
Religion may well be satisfied with this conclusion.

It is not impossible, however, that one may
go a step farther. Even our mathematical dem-
onstrations depend at every step upon the certainty of intuitive insight, and it is quite possible
that Schopenhauer was right in asserting that
so-called mathematical proofs are simply our
labored attempted justifications of insights in-
tuitively certain; that we see first, and prove
afterward; we do not prove and then see. In
a quite similar sense, it may be, that with as
real a certainty as our natures can give us anything, God is given, in the two fundamental
assumptions which have been seen to be implicit
in all our thought and life, for they are neces-
sities of thought and life; we seem really to use
them in all subordinate thinking, as clearly
given certainties, much as we use our mathematical insights. The precise way in which
we come to these certainties may be hidden from
us in both cases, but they are not counted less
certain on that account. Such added logical
obscurity as seems to attach to this immediate
practical certainty of God has been perhaps

sufficiently accounted for. There are weighty reasons why the real immediate certainty of God, upon which we seem to be perpetually counting in all life and thought, should not reveal itself at once to our seeming. The certainty given us is like that of the moral life. So far, as to the theistic argument.

AS TO THE PERSONAL RELATION TO GOD

XXXII

THE NEED OF THE MODERN MAN MET ONLY IN CHRIST

Surely Herrmann is right in saying that theologians of all schools may at least agree as to the general meaning of personal Christianity. "It is a communion of the soul with the living God, through the mediation of Christ. Herein is really included all that belongs to the characteristic life of Christendom—revelation and faith, conversion and the comfort of forgiveness, the joy of faith and the service of love, lonely communion with God, and life in Christian fellowship."[1]

Our very first and greatest problem, therefore, on the positive side, in dealing with the reality of the spiritual life, is to make it clear just how the individual soul may come into undoubted communion with a living God. It needs especially to be noted that our age has come, in such preëminent degree, to scientific and moral self-consciousness, that for the men of to-day the previous easier roads into the religious life are in large degree closed. The

[1] Herrmann, *Communion with God,* Second English edition, p. 9.

psychological treatment, for example, of mystical experiences has made it impossible for us to take at their own estimation all kinds of ecstatic states, and we can feel no surety in these short-cuts to communion with God in a religious experience that cannot bear a rational and ethical test. With Herrmann, we have to ask those who so base their religious conviction, "how they are sure they are really aware of God Himself when they have those emotions in which their whole nature seems exalted. Our confidence in God needs other support than the recollection of such purely emotional experiences can give."[1]

Whatever has been true for previous generations, and whatever is still true for those who have not entered fully into the consciousness of the present time—for many of us, our road to God must now be indubitably rational and ethical. It is impossible that we should rest in any religious experience that cannot so justify itself. The men of the fully modern spirit are, therefore, simply driven to find their way into a personal communion with God through facts so great that they can bear the severest rational and ethical test. And the religion that can fully satisfy the modern man

[1] *Op. cit.* p. 36.

must, thus, build unmistakably on the great fact-foundation of man's own rational and ethical nature, and upon a personality great enough to reveal God, and to bring indubitable conviction of God's existence and of his personal communion with the individual soul.

It is just at this point that Christianity has its supreme gift to make to the man of to-day. For the service of Christianity here is the more priceless and indispensable to the modern man, the more deeply he has entered into the modern spirit. For the deeper our moral consciousness, the greater our sense of moral need. In Herrmann's words,[1] "We feel ourselves to be separated from God, and consequently crippled in our faith by things which troubled the ancients very little. We cannot go back to our first simple indifference to moral demands after our conscience has once been sensible of them. Above all, the knowledge that we are bound to unconditional obedience can never die away into sloth and inactivity after it has once dawned upon us. So that when we are faced by something that wants to force itself on us as a Power over our entire life, the doubt arises in our minds whether in it we really find something we can be conscientiously willing to obey un-

[1] *Op. cit.* p. 63.

conditionally. He who is morally free will mock at a religion that is above morality just as he pities one that is beneath it. Therefore, the only God that can reveal Himself to us is one who shows Himself to us in our moral struggle as the Power to which our souls are really subject. This is what is vouchsafed to us in the revelation of God in Jesus Christ." This simply means that, for the modern man who has awakened to full moral self-consciousness, many an ancient way of approach to God is decisively closed; and if he is to come into communion with God at all, it must be by a manifestation of God great enough to make certain both the holiness of God and his forgiveness of us.

Now, it is through the witness of the New Testament writers that we find in Christ for ourselves a fact so great, so transcendent, that we come back to it again and again with calm assurance, to find in its simple presence the indubitable conviction of the spiritual world, of our own intended destiny, of God, and of his holiness and his love. Christ does not merely tell us these things—he does much more— he makes us *able to believe* them. He, and no other as he, searches us, humbles us, assures us, and exalts us at the same time. Only through him do we come with assurance into the great con-

victions, the great hopes, and the great aspirations; and these measure us as does nothing
else.   Only through him are we brought into
living communion with the living God.   If I
may quote Herrmann again: "The most important thing for the man who is to submit himself to God is surely that he should be absolutely
certain of the reality of God, and Jesus does
establish in us, through the fact of his personal
life, a certainty of God which covers every
doubt.   When once he has attracted us by the
beauty of His Person, and made us bow before
Him by its exalted character, then even amid
our deepest doubts, that Person of Jesus will
remain present with us as a thing incomparable,
the most precious fact in history, the most
precious fact our life contains."   Thus, "the
religious life of the Christian is inseparable
from vision of the personal life of Jesus.   That
vision must be the Christian's constant com-
panion, and so it is, as he finds more and more
that in such vision he grasps that reality without
which all else in the world is empty and deso-
late."

XXXIII

THE NEEDED EMPHASES IN MODERN RELIGIOUS LIFE

If one asks, now, what is involved in these statements, and attempts to characterize the Christian way to communion with God, he will be obliged to say that, for the fully modern man, the way must be ethical, Christian, social, biblical, practical, and, in all these points alike, rational.

It must be ethical, for no religious experience can justify itself to a man who has come to moral self-consciousness, which does not offer, in the sphere of the moral, a deepening of the moral life. Mere emotions, therefore, however entrancing, will not answer. Here lies the far reaching significance of the Reformers' insistence that God's presence is to be found in the daily calling, and the sense of his nearness to be won just there, *in* the doing of the daily duty.

It must be Christian, in building, as we have seen, directly on the fact of Christ as the one fact sufficiently great and significant to open a certain way to God for the modern man.

It must be social, because in the sphere of

religion, as in all other spheres of value, we are almost inevitably introduced through the witness of those who already share in the value. And, doubtless, for some the religious experience remains to the end in much larger degree indirect, than for others. And for all of us some of our best visions of the spiritual come through others. The social trend of the Christian's communion with God is seen, too, in the indispensable fellowship with the Church and with the great prophetic seers of history, as well as in the inevitable way in which the kingdom of God must go forward by the witness, given from heart to heart, of what men have found Chirst to be to them.

It must be biblical, not as building on a book, but in just so far as the Bible is regarded not as a record of doctrines or history to be authoritatively accepted, but as a book of honest testimony to experience. Its supreme value lies just here. For the testimony of another is our chief road to enlargement of life. Most of all, it is through such simple, honest witness that the New Testament puts us face to face with the redeeming personality of Christ. Whatever our theories about the Bible, it is not as compelling authority, but as simple, honest witness that the New Testament brings us emancipating power.

In another's words, "The inner life of Jesus is stamped on the testimony of men who have been set free by him. In this way has it become a force in history, and in no other way was that possible. Hence we can lay hold on it and make it ours only when we let the witness of his disciples lay hold on us." And that witness the Christian "finds in Scripture as nowhere else."

Treated as a book throbbing thus with personal life—as a book of honest testimony to experience broad and deep, in the moral and spiritual life—and approached through a true historical method, I have no doubt that the Bible will increasingly prove what the free critic, Edmond Scherer, claimed: "The Bible will ever be the book of power, the marvellous book, *the* book above all others. It will ever be the light of the mind and the bread of the soul. Neither the superstitions of some, nor the irreligious negations of others have been able to do it harm. If there is anything certain in the world, it is that the destinies of the Bible are linked with the destinies of holiness on earth."

The modern emphasis, again, must be practical, as wrought out in experience, and submitting not only gladly, but of deliberate purpose, to the test of experiment in life. The experiment here is the endeavor to find whether the deepest laws and trends of our being do unmistakably point to God.   And it is in this practical way that we must apply, each for himself, the psychological and sociological tests which have already been considered.   Do the Christian conception of the spiritual life and the honest response to the inner life of Christ give opportunity for the highest and fullest personal self-expression and personal association, justifying themselves, thus, rationally and ethically?   If the individual finds himself compelled, as I certainly do, to return an unhesitating affirmative to this question, then he will simply be saying that the deepest laws and trends of human nature reach their fullest justification and growth only upon the Christian assumption.

XXXIV.

THE METHOD OF THE SPIRITUAL LIFE

The consideration of these needed emphases in modern religious life, itself, suggests the two great positive ways, already considered, of coming into assured personal relation to God. They are not really two ways, but rather two aspects of our one great method of finding the reality of the spiritual.

Starting from the analogy of the way in which we come into all the great values of life, we may say that to have a real and significant spiritual life simply requires that we should put ourselves in the presence of the greatest facts of the spiritual world, in voluntary surrender to them, just so far as they command our inner allegiance. This will mean, above all, that we put ourselves steadily, persistently into the closest possible relation with the inner life of Christ, giving that life full opportunity to make upon us its own legitimate impression, to communicate to us Christ's own sense of the reality of God and of the spiritual life. Only so shall we be following the prime law for coming into all the greatest values of life—staying persistently in the presence of the best we know in the realm of the spiritual, with honest response to its natural, inevitable appeal. This will bring us surely, increasingly, into Christ's life of love to God and love to men. We need here particularly to remember how inextricably the sense of the reality of the spiritual is bound up with persistent loyalty to the ethical demands, just so far as known.

Starting from the analogy of personal relations, we may say that to have a real and significant spiritual life requires that we should honestly recognize that the spiritual life is essentially a life of personal relations with men and with God, and should act accordingly. That is, we must simply follow the laws of the spiritual life. This means that we must steadily fulfil the conditions of a deepening personal relation with God and with men; only being sure that we do not transfer to God the limitations of the finite. The conditions of the spiritual life can thus be pointed out, and fulfilled, and we may count upon the result. Every bit of experience in the human relations throws light upon the divine; all growth in the divine life is immediate gain for the human relations. The ethical and religious are bound up together, and all life becomes one—a life of learning to love.

15

This is simply putting to practical test Christ's hypothesis of love as the essence of life. The method confronts us, that is, with the plain challenge: Go forward, in your religious life, in steady fulfilment of the conditions of a deepening personal relation man-ward and God-ward, and you will find the relation to God becoming increasingly real and satisfying. But as soon as one seeks honestly to carry out this counsel in relation to God, he sees at once that every deepening personal relation requires mutual self-revelation on the part of the persons concerned. He will seek, therefore, to build the relation to God upon the fullest revelation of God. This he must naturally find in the world's most significant personality, Christ; and in the presence of that completest self-revelation of God, he goes forward in his fulfilment of the conditions of a deepening friendship with God.

The two methods, thus, both necessarily build upon close and persistent association with the life of Christ, as the greatest spiritual fact of the world, and the most significant self-revelation of God. Both emphasize the need of honest response to the best we know. Both count upon the appeal and the inevitable contagion of Christ's own life. But the laws of the growing life are most clearly and definitely indicated as those of a deepening personal relation.[1]

[1] Attention may well be called just here to the peculiar value of Drummond's address on "The Changed Life" as at least a partial illustration of the use of both methods.

AS TO PARTICULAR CHRISTIAN DOCTRINES

XXXV

DOCTRINE AS EXPRESSION OF EXPERIENCE WITH CHRIST

If one turns, now, in the third place, in fulfilment of the positive problem of seeking reality for the spiritual life, from the rational argument for the existence of God, and the problem of personal relation to God, to ask for the way in which single Christian doctrines may become to him most real, he must see that this can be possible for the modern man only as these individual doctrines are associated in the closest way with assured fact and undoubted personal experience.

Has not the time fully come when we are to say unhesitatingly that any manual of vital and even true theology must be, at the same time, a manual of practical religion? For in any inquiry concerning single Christian doctrines, we are only asking: What does such an assured relation to God in Christ, in the realm of the morally infinite, mean as to God, as to Christ, as to men and their redemption? The individual doctrines, that is, must grow directly out of the individual's experience of communion with God; grow without pretense, and in all honesty, yet with modest open-mindedness as to the experience of others, just as one tries to keep both this honest and modest attitude in the realm of art and literary criticism.

The individual doctrine, too, must not only grow naturally out of the individual's own experience, but, based on that experience, it must come to the man with assured conviction. In the revelation of God in Christ, the Christian must see that he has relation to undoubted fact. And that means, first, that he must find in Christ not merely—what he may be thoroughly convinced that he finds in the case of a given portrait or story—a sure reflex of life, but, rather, the sense of God as *now* reaching him in Christ, because the inner spirit of the life of Christ is found to be in the highest degree rational and ethical, both in itself and in its implications.

And the Christian conviction means, in the second place, that the Christian finds in Christ, again, not merely that which he feels that he could not produce out of his own resources, as one has said, but rather that he finds in Christ the present, undoubted assurance and call of God and the spiritual world, just as, upon the

Christian view, we feel the will of God in every demand of duty.

It follows that those doctrines will seem to us inevitable and Christian, which grow, in just this indubitable and individual way, out of a communion with God which we cannot question. But this will also mean, in turn, that, while doubtless certain Christian doctrines follow more directly than others from the Christian experience, we shall not be able consistently to draw hard and fast lines between the doctrines, as the full followers of Ritschl seem inclined to do. If doctrine is simply the outcome and expression of experience, then what we shall be able to reach in doctrine will depend upon the breadth and depth of our experience. It would be hazardous, for example, for us to set the exact limit of assured doctrine that might grow out of the depth and clearness of the consciousness of Christ. And with every true Christian we are dealing with growing life. Therefore, upon the very conception of doctrine which we are urging, the growing life ought to mean growing doctrine.

Is Herrmann, for example, perfectly clear as to the lines of separation between those doctrines which are a direct expression of a personal experience of God's self-revelation to

us in Christ, and those which are "a thought
or doctrine arising from and expressing faith
in our redemption," and those which he regards
as speculative additions (as the preëxistence of
Christ, theories of the atonement, etc.)? And
where do we find the doctrines, which express
the consciousness that "the Christian life contains depths which cannot be fathomed," and
those which are "corollaries" from Christian
experience? Are his distinctions clear? On
his own theory, can he be so sure in the drawing of these sharp lines? Is it not quite certain
that some doctrines would seem speculative for
some, and for others will seem to be directly
connected with their experience? And there
will be, likewise, differences for the same individual at different periods in his growth. May
not growing experience of the meaning of
Christ make some further propositions seem like
immediate expressions of one's faith? Let one
think, for example, of the way in which John
and Paul both seem to have come to their
thought of Christ's preëxistence; or, still better,
if the doctrine is to be ascribed to Christ himself, of the way in which we may suppose it
arose in Christ's own consciousness.

In this attempt to express in rational and
definite statements the content of the Christian

experience, it seems evident that we must make our ideal at least a final unity; though this final unity, doubtless, is to be sought with the most careful avoidance of common and serious errors at this point. That is, in the endeavor after unity in his own thought-expression of his Christian faith, one must steadily avoid the mistakes of dogmatism concerning any single doctrine, of putting all doctrines on a level, of making all those doctrines of various degrees, which we seem to ourselves to have reached, into a test for others, and especially of using any doctrinal statements as a way to life, instead of simply the expression of the life already there.

As to this last point, however, the Christian needs continually to remember that life, too, grows through clear and definite expression, even in thought; although, no doubt, in life and its complex experience there is much that must always transcend such expression. But it is a lazy, and in my judgment a finally immoral, way for the Christian simply to rest back upon a more or less emotional experience, which he refuses to try, either for himself or for others, to express in clear and definite thought as well as in action.

Once more, with reference to all the individual doctrines we should be able in much to cut under questions of merely historical criticism, or of philosophical speculation, in recognition both of the fundamental likeness and of the unique contribution of the Christian experience, through undoubted relation to fact in that experience.

Let us ask, then, just how certainty might come to one, as to any doctrine, through the facts of his religious experience.

XXXVI

ILLUSTRATED IN THE DOCTRINE OF PERSONAL IMMORTALITY

To take a single example, how has Christ really proved himself to be the one great source of faith in immortality, just as he is the great source of our idea of God and of our faith in God? What, indeed, in this modern day is the ground of the hope of immortality for most of those who hold it vitally and strongly? In simple truth it would seem that the answer to this last question must be that the primary ground of our hope is in Christ, not in philosophy, not in science, not in any other religion. These may or may not seem corroborative. But, in any case, we do not build primarily upon them. They are simply not able to give that certain conviction for which we seek.

Harnack's statement upon this point can hardly be doubted: "Whatever may have happened at the grave [of Christ] and in the matter of the appearances, one thing is certain: *This grave was the birthplace of the indestructible belief that death is vanquished, that there is a life eternal.* It is useless to cite Plato; it is useless to point to the Persian religion, and the ideas and literature of later Judaism. All that would have perished and has perished; but the certainty of the resurrection and of a life eternal which is bound up with the grave in Joseph's garden has not perished, and on the conviction that *Jesus lives* we still base those hopes of citizenship in an Eternal City which make our earthly life worth living and tolerable. 'He delivered them who through fear of death were all their lifetime subject to bondage,' as the writer of the epistle to the Hebrews confesses. That is the point. And although there be exceptions to its sway, wherever, despite all the weight of nature, there is a strong faith in the infinite value of the soul; wherever death has lost its terrors; wherever the sufferings of the present are measured against a future of glory, this feeling of life is bound up with the conviction that Jesus Christ has passed through death, that God has awakened him and raised him to life and glory."[1]

If in fact, then, the great ground of our faith in immortality is the personality of Christ, let us ask further, Why is it Christ? Just how is it that our faith in immortality builds so directly upon him? Not because Christ has much to

[1] *What is Christianity?* p. 162.

say about heavenly rewards; not because of much direct teaching; though giving, I think, straightforward assurance, he has, in fact, done little to satisfy our insatiate curiosity here. Not primarily, either, because of the resurrection evidence, however we may estimate that. For myself, for reasons into which I need not here go, I think there are more difficulties in setting aside the plain New Testament belief in the objective resurrection of Christ than most of our critics seem to realize. I have small faith in a gospel emptied of facts. And I share here Professor Mathews' expressed conviction of the genuine religious value of the historical fact of the resurrection.[1] But, at the same time, I cannot doubt that we cannot and do not build our faith in immortality primarily upon the historical evidence for the bodily resurrection of Jesus, even where we are able fully to accept it. We do not believe in Christ's Lordship over life and death because we believe in the historical evidence for his resurrection. Rather this evidence has with us the weight it does, because we are already convinced of his Lordship in the moral and spiritual world.

Our faith in immortality, that is, is built

[1] See his very suggestive Chapter III, in *The Church and the Changing Order,* pp. 47 ff.

directly upon Christ, just because of the spirit of his life. He seems himself to live in the very atmosphere of the assurance of immortality, in the atmosphere of eternity. He expects it. He cannot be disappointed, we feel. But, more than that, eternity fits into that most perfect life of trust and love. It is harmonious with it. His life seems to us to have an eternal quality. We cannot think of it as of merely temporary significance. It must abide.

And so Harnack seems justified in continuing: "What else can we believe but that the earliest disciples also found the ultimate foundation of their faith in the living Lord to be the strength which had gone out from him? It was a life never to be destroyed which they felt to be going out from him; only for a brief span of time could his death stagger them; the strength of the Lord prevailed over everything; God did not give him over to death; he lives as the first-fruits of those who have fallen asleep. It is not by any speculative ideas of philosophy but by the vision of Jesus' life and death and by the feeling of his imperishable union with God that mankind, so far as it believes in these things, has attained to that certainty of eternal life for which it was meant, and which it dimly discerns—eternal life in time and beyond time.

This feeling first established faith in the value of personal life. But of every attempt to demonstrate the certainty of 'immortality' by logical process, we may say in the words of the poet:

> 'Believe and venture: as for pledges,
> The gods give none.'

Belief in the living Lord and in a life eternal is the *act* of the freedom which is born of God."[1]

To like import, Matheson speaks of "the impossible consequences of a denied future." "If there be no immortality, Christ is dead—the purest, the fairest, the loveliest life that ever breathed has become less than the napkin, less than the grave-clothes, less than the sepulchre.' It is to Paul an impossible consequence. He cannot think of Christ as dead. He says, 'If Christ be dead, death must be a delusion.' Did you never feel this experience? You parted with a friend an hour ago, and the next hour you heard that he was dead; you said 'Impossible!' And when it was confirmed, you said again 'Impossible! if he be dead, then death is not to die. I must have misnamed it, misread it, mistaken the inscription on its doorway. Death henceforth is a gate of life to me.'

"Son of Man, whenever I doubt of life, I think of Thee. Nothing is so impossible as that

[1] *Op. cit.* p. 163.

16

Thou shouldst be dead. I can imagine the hills to dissolve in vapor, and the stars to melt in smoke, and the rivers to empty themselves in sheer exhaustion; but I feel no limit in Thee. Thou never growest old to me. Last century is old, last year is old, last season is an obsolete fashion; but Thou art not obsolete. Thou art abreast of all the centuries, nay, Thou goest before them like the star. I have never come up with Thee, modern as I am. Thy picture is at home in every land. A thousand have fallen at its side, but it has kept its bloom; old Jerusalem, old Rome, new Rome—it has been young amid them all. Therefore, when oppressed by the sight of death, I shall turn to Thee. I shall see my immortality in Thee. I shall read the possibilities of my soul in Thee. I shall measure the promise of my manhood by Thee. I shall comfort myself by the impossible conclusion 'If there be no immortality, Christ is dead.' "

We build, then, first of all and chiefly, upon the essential spirit of Christ's own life. And we find this sense of the immediate perception of the eternal quality of the life of Christ confirming our faith in our own immortality, because this undeniable quality in his life means that he is the supreme artist in living, and that we have reason, therefore, to trust his moral and spiritual sanity and insight, both for himself and for others.

We remind ourselves, besides, of his express assurance. The eschatological note in the teaching of Jesus, whether urged as a reproach or as praise, seems, in any case, unmistakable. It is hard to see how one can question that the teaching of Jesus looks to a future life for his disciples as well as for himself. And this express assurance, coming from such a personality as Christ's, deservedly carries the greatest weight.

And, when one turns to the different elements in the teaching of Jesus, he not only finds nothing inharmonious with this conviction of the immortal life, but every bit of the rest of the teaching seems rather to demand it. His one great central message of God as Father requires it. For that would seem first of all to mean that our life, as children of God, is in him and must deepen as our personal relation to him deepens. Quite surely, as Münsterberg contends, one does not care for mere extension in space as dead space, nor for senseless extension in time, like changeless stones. But that seems to me a rather barren concession, and not at all to settle the question of the value of a continued, steadily deepening, ever more and more significant personal relation to God and to

other persons. Has the life so far been of value?
Then I am quite unable to understand how it
can be thought that its continuance can mean
nothing.

What is, indeed, the meaning of the eternal
God as Father, if there are no abiding children?
Is it not right into this depth that Christ looks,
when he says, "God is not the God of the dead,
but of the living"? The Father cannot mock
his children, and cannot disappoint them. His
own life is the eternal life, and it is the very
center of Christ's teaching that God opens the
sharing of exactly that life to all his children.

And, again, is it not of the essence of Christ's
message as a *gospel* that it is tidings of the
eternal, that it is assurance of the abiding, as
over against the temporal and passing? "He
that doeth the will of God abideth forever."
Is Christ's message not good news, just for the
reason that it opens a personal relation to the
eternal God, and that man's life, therefore, is
knit up with the very life of the Eternal?

Christ's ethical insistence, moreover, his appeal to the individual sense of responsibility and
accountability, his summing up of the law and
of all religion and of all life in love—what is
all this but just so much repeated emphasis
on the essential significance of the individual

personality, without which none of these things are possible? What does character itself mean, else? And how can one assert the eternal nature of the ethical, without at the same time asserting the enduring existence of individual persons?

How closely our faith in immortality is linked with the ethical, may be seen in the fact that the immortal hope is likely to go up or down in us with our own moral state. When our life is most surely of the quality that ought to endure, we find it easier to believe in immortality. And it is exactly through Christ, it should be noted, that we are chiefly and most surely brought on into character and into belief in it. Thus, just because Christ has not only within himself a character which has the quality of the eternal, and a teaching which implies at every point the immortal life, but because he is himself the one supreme inspirer to character, is our faith in immortality connected directly with Christ.

Christ's doctrine of unlimited self-sacrifice is another element of his teaching which implies most assuredly the abiding value of men. For there is simply no way of rationally justifying either the prodigal pouring out of his own life, or that which he demands from others, except upon the assumption of the abiding and inestimable value of men as children of God, as beings who can look forward to a life to whose growth in breadth and significance no limits can be put.

Everywhere, that is, in Christ's teaching one strikes the eternal note, that means nothing except as an appeal to an abiding personality. What meaning can it have for men, and what meaning in harmony with the teaching of Christ, that some impersonal outcome is left or lost in the Infinite? Who cares, whether God or man? The only essential significance of life we know lies in personal relations. What could be the will result, the character result, apart from continuing individual personality in the sense of a genuine self-consciousness and of individual initiative?

The real ground, thus, of faith in immortality is Christ himself, his character, his teaching, his death. Our faith does not primarily depend on what we can persuade ourselves to believe about the resurrection and its evidence, significant as I believe that to be. Quite independently of that, we feel forced to believe that Christ has the power of the endless life in him, in any case; and this way of getting at it is open to all, and means life and the assurance of a direct relation with the living God. There is, thus, a very real sense in which we are able, through the majesty of the inner spirit of Christ himself,

as revealed in the entire sweep of his life and
verified in present experience, to cut under all
questions of merely historical criticism, that can
reasonably be regarded as at all open, or of
philosophical speculation, and to reach an assurance grounded as deeply as assurance can be
grounded, in the strength of our own rational
and ethical convictions as we face the fact of
Christ. Is faith in immortality an outworn
belief? If so, how does it come to be bound
up so indissolubly with the transcendent living,
and the transcendent moral and spiritual insight
of Christ?

So Harnack can say:[1] "I admit that if historical research had proved that he was an
apocalyptic enthusiast or visionary, whose image
and utterances were advanced to the level of
pure aim and lofty thought only by the refining
influence of later times, it would be another
matter. But who has proved that, and who
could prove it? For besides the four written
Gospels, we possess a fifth, unwritten; and in
many respects its voice is clearer and more
effective than those of the other four—I mean
the united testimony of the first Christian community. It enables us to gather what was the
prevailing impression made by this personality,

[1] *Christianity and History*, pp. 56-59.

and in what sense his disciples understood his words and the testimony which he gave of himself. It is true that his clothes—the outward form of his doctrine—were part of the heritage; but the great and simple truths which he came to preach, the personal sacrifice which he made, and his victory in death, were what formed the new life of his community; and when the apostle Paul with divine power described this life as a life in the Spirit, and again as a life in love, he was only giving back the light which had dawned upon him in and through Jesus Christ his Lord. This is a simple matter of fact, which no historical criticism can in any way alter. All that it can do is to place it in a clearer light, and so increase our reverence for the divinity which was revealed in radiance in a Son of Abraham, amid the wreck and refuse of a narrow world. Let the plain Bible-reader continue to read his Gospels as he has hitherto read them; for in the end the critic cannot read them otherwise. What the one regards as their true gist and meaning, the other must acknowledge to be such. But the facts, the facts! I do not know how there can be a greater fact than the one which I have just been describing. By the side of it, what can any historical detail signify?"

Harnack thus suggests that, standing upon a broad basis of secure historical fact, one may find the personality of Christ continually verifying itself to him anew, through its thoroughgoing consistency with our deepest rational and ethical convictions. That personality "finds" us more surely than any other fact of the world; fits, as does no other, the highest and worthiest in us. Greater proof than this it is hard to ask, or to give.

In Harnack's words, once more:[1] "Eighteen hundred years separate us from this history; but if we seriously ask ourselves what it is that has given us the courage to believe that in the history of the world God prevails, not only by moral and intellectual forces, but by His presence in the midst of it; if we ask what it is that leads us to believe in an eternal life—our answer is, that we make bold to believe it in reliance upon Christ. *Jesus lives, and with him I live also.* He is the firstborn among many brothers; he is our surety for the reality of a future world. So it is, then, that God speaks to us through him. It was testified of Christ that he was the *Way,* the *Truth,* and the *Life;* as such he is still revealed to our inmost feeling, and therein consists his presence to us. As

[1] *Op. cit.* pp. 48-49.

surely as everything depends on the soul finding God and becoming one with Him, so surely is he the true Saviour, Guide, and Lord who leads the soul to God."

It is by some such road as this, without ignoring in any way the value of corroborative lines of reasoning, that the man of the simple Christian life, who is neither historical and literary critic, or scientist, or philosopher, may find his way, by a road genuinely rational and genuinely ethical, into the very presence of God, and into the assurance of the greatest facts and doctrines of the spiritual life. This road is not a way to be travelled only by the ingenious reasoner; many a simple and unlearned soul has trod it confidently, even though unconsciously. It has been for him, as it must ultimately be for us all, not so much a matter of subtle inference, as of immediate and direct spiritual perception. He has found in Christ his Lord so great a fact, that all else that is much worth while is given him in Christ. And his argument, if he has one, is the very simple one of Paul, "How shall He not also with him freely give us all things?"

INDEX

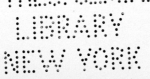

By the
Rev. WALTER RAUSCHENBUSCH

Professor of Church History in Rochester Theological Seminary

Christianity and the Social Crisis

"It is of the sort to make its readers feel that the book was bravely written to free an honest man's heart; that conscientious scholarship, hard thinking, and the determination to tell the truth as he sees it, have wrought it out and enriched it; that it is written in a clear, incisive style; that stern passion and gentle sentiment stir at times among the words, and keen wit and grim humor flash here and there in the turn of a sentence; and that there is a noble end in view. If the hope be too confident, if there be once in a while a step taken beyond the line of justice into indignation, if a quaint old prejudice or even animosity bustles to the front in an emergency—no matter. It is a book to like, to learn from, and, though the theme be sad and serious, to be charmed with."—*N. Y. Times' Sat. Review of Books*.

Cloth, 12mo, $1.50 net

By the Rev. SHAILER MATHEWS

Professor of New Testament History and Interpretation in the University of Chicago

The Church and the Changing Order

". . . a most interesting and valuable contribution to the literature of a subject that is growing in popular attention every day. While among the deeply, really religious and genuinely scientific there is no conflict or antagonism where even there is not accord, thus unfortunately is not commonly the case among the masses who have only caught the forms of religious and scientific knowledge without their spirit. This book is addressed much more it seems to the religious than the scientific, possibly because the latter have the less need for repentance. Those who are troubled in any way at the seeming conflict between the demands of faith, on the one hand, and the experiences of their own reason and the problems of modern, social and industrial life will find here much sage, illuminating, and practical counsel."—*Evening Post*.

Cloth, 12mo, $1.50 net

THE MACMILLAN COMPANY
Publishers, 64-66 Fifth Avenue, NEW YORK   5123